The Poetics of Yury Olesha

University of Florida Monographs
Humanities Number 63

The Poetics of Yury Olesha

Victor Peppard

University of Florida Press
Gainesville

Library of Congress Cataloging-in-Publication Data

Peppard, Victor.
    The poetics of Yury Olesha / Victor Peppard. —1st ed.
      p.   cm. — (University of Florida humanities monographs; 63)
    Bibliography : p.
    Includes index.
    ISBN 0-8130-0950-2 (alk. paper)
    1. Olesha, IUrii Karlovich, 1899–1960—Criticism and interpretation. I.Title. II.
Series: University of Florida monographs. Humanities ; no. 63.
PG3476.O37Z78 1989
891.78′4209—dc20   89-33166
                                                                               CIP

The University of Florida Press is a member of University Presses of Florida, the
scholarly publishing agency of the State University System of Florida. Books are
selected for publication by faculty editorial committees at each of Florida's nine
public universities: Florida A&M University (Tallahassee), Florida Atlantic University (Boca Raton), Florida International University (Miami), Florida State University
(Tallahassee), University of Central Florida (Orlando), University of Florida (Gainesville), University of North Florida (Jacksonville), University of South Florida (Tampa),
University of West Florida (Pensacola).
    Orders for books published by all member presses should be addressed to Univer-
sity Presses of Florida, 15 NW 15th Street, Gainesville, FL 32603.

To family and friends who made it possible
when I wasn't.

Contents

Acknowledgments

THE research for this book was aided by grants from the National Endowment for the Humanities and the Arts and Letters Research Council of the University of South Florida. The Russian Research Laboratory and the staff of the Slavic and East European Library of the University of Illinois, Champaign-Urbana, provided invaluable support and assistance over the course of several summers. I would particularly like to thank June Pachuta Farris and Irina Fainzelberg for helping me to assemble bibliographic material on Olesha. The Interlibrary Loan Department of the University of South Florida Library was also most helpful and cooperative.

I am grateful to editor Kenneth N. Brostrom for allowing me to use material from my article "Olesha's *Envy* and the Carnival," *Papers in Slavic Philology* 4 (Ann Arbor: Department of Slavic Languages and Literatures, University of Michigan, 1984), 179–89, in altered form in this book and editor Boris A. Sorokin for letting me use here material from my article "Olesha's *No Day without a Line*: A New Genre or an Old Trick?" *Proceedings of the Kentucky Foreign Language Conference 1985: Slavic Section* 3 (Lexington: Department of Slavic and Oriental Languages, University of Kentucky), 92–98.

Valenty Cukierman was especially generous in allowing me to use the extensive materials he has gathered in his research on Odessan writers, including in particular material from the archive of G. I. Dolinov from the Saltykov-Shchedrin Public Library in Leningrad and material from Olesha's archive in Tsentral'nyi Gosudarstvennyi Arkhiv Literatury i Iskusstava in Moscow. I would also like to express my gratitude to Elizabeth Beaujour and Robert Szulkin for making their work on Olesha available to me.

Gary Saul Morson provided me with invaluable assistance in the form of his extremely thorough and insightful reading of my manuscript. I have made wide use of his numerous and perceptive suggestions. Michael Zelina was good enough to help with bibliographic data at a strategic moment. And I would like to thank Michael Massey for his assistance in bringing me into the computer age.

Finally, I want to give a very special thanks to Pat Schuster for the superb work and unfailing good spirits she showed in preparing the manuscript at all stages.

Note on Transliteration

THE basic system of transliteration used in this book is that of the Library of Congress, with "ya" and "yu" in initial position instead of "ia" and "iu." The letter "y" is also used in surnames ending in "-sky" and in first names familiar in English, such as "Valya" and "Volodya." Well-known names such as Dostoevsky, Meyerhold, and Mayakovsky are left in their familiar variants throughout.

Introduction /
Life and Carnival

SELDOM has a writer who published so few major works produced so many enduring controversies as Yury Olesha. Olesha, who was born in 1899 and died in 1960, held a position of prominence in Russian literature mainly in the late 1920s and 1930s, but the debate over him that began with the publication of his novel *Envy* (*Zavist'*) in 1927 continues apace more than a quarter century after his death.

Opinions about Olesha are remarkably divergent. To some he was a painstaking craftsman who had a mania for perfection that prevented him from producing the volume of work that might have been expected of such a talented writer. To others he was a lazybones, a chatterer, and a drinker who lacked the discipline to finish what he had started. The predominant view of Olesha among his contemporaries holds that he was an enchanting raconteur and a gifted, gnome-like character who charmed all those who came in contact with him. Others consider him to have been a nasty, spiteful man with an acid tongue who often needlessly hurt those who were close to him.[1]

Opinions on the significance of Olesha's literary output have been no less divided. In the West there has been a tendency to view him as something of an undeclared rebel who suffered persecution for his unorthodox artistic methods and chose silence rather than compromise when his favorite themes and techniques fell out of favor but who left a brilliant if small literary legacy.[2] This view is supported by some of Olesha's contemporaries, among them Emmanuel Kazakevich, who believes that Olesha "never wrote what he did not think, and what he was not in agreement with he did not write about at all. . . . He will be an example of . . . the indisputable absence of artistic compromise."[3] Another contemporary of Olesha, Arkady Belinkov, who knew Olesha well, has written an extensive study whose purpose is to discredit Olesha as a timeserver who gladly went along with the demands of the Soviet authorities and contributed nothing of special merit or innovation to the corpus of Russian literature. Belinkov even accuses Olesha of being a notorious betrayer of the Soviet intelligentsia under Stalin.[4]

While Olesha was a genuinely complex, contradictory person, and both he and his contemporaries were fond of cultivating an enigmatic aura about him, it is possible to penetrate most of the myths and the mystique that have surrounded him for so long. In some cases the partisans of Olesha's image as a fairy-tale character of mysterious qualities will be disappointed to discover that prosaic and painful realities often underlie the outward appearance. Nevertheless, Olesha's persistence as an incorrigible fantast is well documented.

Although Olesha has been given extensive critical attention over the years, there are important aspects of his work, especially his poetics, that have not yet been sufficiently recognized or evaluated. In the absence of a comprehensive conception of his poetics, there has been a tendency to view in isolation from one another the salient features of Olesha's work, such as his striking imagery, his provocative thematics, and his distinctive style and narrative technique. There has also been relatively little study of what, if anything, ties Olesha's work together in different forms, genres, and periods. Perhaps most surprisingly, there has been almost no analysis of one of the most remarkable aspects of Olesha's creative output, its markedly carnivalistic tenor and ambience. Furthermore, the fundamentally dialogical quality of Olesha's best works has gone virtually unexamined. The purpose of this study therefore is to demonstrate that there is in fact an identifiable set of interconnected poetic principles that governs Olesha's work and gives it artistic coherence.

Olesha's childhood was distinguished by his excellence as a student and his involvement with sport. As a student in the Rishelevsky Gymnasium in Odessa, Olesha graduated with straight A's and won a gold medal for his performance in language and literature.[5] It was also at the Rishelevsky Gymnasium that Olesha met and played soccer with one of the early stars of Odessan and Russian soccer, Grigory Bogemsky,[6] who was in addition a track athlete of international caliber. Bogemsky's name appears in various places throughout Olesha's life and works. It is possible that Olesha's lifelong fascination with people such as Bogemsky and Mayakovsky, who have a certain star quality, began in his early acquaintance with Bogemsky. Olesha describes his youthful infatuation with Bogemsky in *No Day without a Line* (*Ni dnia bez strochki*) (1965, 1974):

> Even beside the fact that he was a hundred-meter sprint champion, a champion high jumper, and a champion pole vaulter, what he accomplished on the soccer field became a legend. And not only in Odessa, but in Petersburg, in Sweden, in Norway!
>
> Oh, that was one of the most captivating spectacles of my childhood, which cried out together with everyone at that minute, jumped up, and applauded. It wasn't just that he was better than everyone, but that this was truly the emergence of a champion.
>
> Do you really not see the exceptional grace of his appearance, his lightness, his "Just a second!" and now he'll run off, and the whole field will run after him—the crowd, the flags, the clouds, life![7]

In all of Olesha's lyrical passages there is none more rapturous than this one, but several match it when he attempts to capture the ineffable feelings a young boy experiences when he watches his favorite champion sportsman or tries on his first pair of soccer shoes.

Olesha's admiration for another star of early Russian soccer and racing in different kinds of vehicles, Sergei Utochkin, is reflected in the story "The Chain" (*Tsep'*) (1928), where Utochkin is one of the characters. During the various stages of his life Olesha looked up to, even idolized certain contemporaries as models of exceptional accomplishment. In his youth Olesha's idols were Bogemsky and Utochkin.

In the 1920s in Moscow the special object of Olesha's admiration was Mayakovsky. The fact that Olesha knew Mayakovsky reasonably well personally tempered his awe of him only very slightly. When Mayakovsky committed suicide and his friends gathered to console each other, Olesha could not believe how prosaic and utterly lacking in splendor it all was. He had evidently expected some sort of extraordinary feeling, event, or atmosphere to accompany the death of an individual so exceptionally talented as Mayakovsky, and said in disillusionment, "And this is the death of Mayakovsky?"[8]

In later years Olesha's idol was Andrei Starostin, one of Russia's great soccer players. Starostin's career parallels Olesha's in rough outline in that, like Olesha, his youth was spent largely playing soccer and his mature years have been devoted to writing. Olesha regarded Starostin as nothing less than the ideal of masculine beauty.[9] Starostin has reciprocated Olesha's admiration generously, and even in his commentaries on contemporary sport and soccer, he seldom fails to mention Olesha. For Starostin, Olesha's judgments and standards in matters of sport are Scripture.[10]

Olesha's idolization of stars in various areas of endeavor, especially sport and the arts, is related to one of the fundamental qualities of his personality. He not only wanted to be with these people, but he desperately wanted to be one of them. The fact that he always seemed to be on the edges of the charmed circle of celebrities but never quite on the inside was a continual source of frustration. It is no coincidence that some of Olesha's major characters, such as Kavalerov and Ivan Babichev of *Envy*, are portrayed as outsiders who can only observe but not participate in the life of the successful people of the world, such as Andrei Babichev. Kavalerov's expulsion from the airshow as well as his and Ivan's observation of the family of Andrei, Valya, and Volodya from behind a wall are only two of the most poignant examples in *Envy* of their status as outsiders.

Even if he never achieved the heights of fame he dreamed of, Olesha had ways of asserting his own special claim to glory. He sometimes referred to himself and wanted others to call him "King Jerzy Pershy the Great"; and he would remind people, "I am a nobleman, a member of the Shlachta" (the Polish nobility).[11] Olesha's father was in fact an impoverished Polish nobleman who worked in a vodka distillery in Odessa.

Olesha is therefore in a sense an archetype of Eastern Europe's cultural and ethnic crosscurrents. He was born of Polish Catholic parents in the Ukraine, in Elizavetograd, now Kirovograd, raised in prerevolutionary Odessa, and spent most of his adult life in Soviet Moscow.[12] Olesha spoke Russian with what one of his contemporaries perceived as "an imperceptible Lithuanian accent" that gave his speech an elegant quality.[13] Olesha's first tutor in Russian was his Polish grandmother,[14] and she may have had an influence on his speech. Because he reveled in the things that made him stand out from others, such as his piercing, blue eyes and Beethoven-like appearance, he took pride in his rare name, which is related to the Russian word for "deer" (*olen'*).[15]

After the Revolution, Olesha's mother and father lived in the town of Grodno, then part of Poland. Although he does not appear to have been very close to his parents, especially his father, who had little time for him as a youth, he felt badly about not visiting them as an adult. Olesha thought that it would be somehow inappropriate simply to go to them and say that he was a writer. "I'll go to them when I have fame and a lot of money, so that the whole town will say: 'The Oleshas' son has arrived.' "[16] This plan, like so many of his others, never materialized, and he never did make the triumphant return to his family that he had fantasized about.

Olesha's early years in Odessa shaped his world view and his literary work in both obvious and subtle ways. The Odessa that he describes in his stories is for the most part very different from the Odessa of his contemporary Isaac Babel. The reader gets only an indirect, almost abstract view of Odessa through the eyes of Olesha's autobiographical narrators in stories such as "The Chain," "I Look into the Past" (*Ya smotriu v proshloe*) (1929), and "Human Material" (*Chelovecheskii material*) (1929), who are preoccupied with their private experiences. In many of Babel's stories about Odessa, the focus is also on the narrator's youthful experiences. Babel, in contrast with Olesha, loves to evoke the local color of Odessa, especially in his descriptions of the life of Odessan Jews and the Odessan underworld of figures such as Benya Krik.[17]

Unlike Babel, Olesha does not employ the special Odessan slang in his characters' speech. It is only in *No Day without a Line* that Odessa really comes to life in Olesha's work. Here he dwells at considerable length on many of the *realia* of prerevolutionary life in Odessa. *No Day* is sprinkled with detailed descriptions of places that give a vivid picture of petty mercantile activity in Odessa before the Revolution—such as the tobacco shop where as a schoolboy Olesha bought school supplies and Roman candles.[18]

One other area of Olesha's work connected with Odessa is worth noting. This is a cycle of poems called "Verses about Odessa" (*Stikhi ob Odesse*) (1917), in which he describes Odessa at different times of year. At this time he also wrote a cycle of poems on themes from Pushkin's work. While Olesha's poetry of this time is largely imitative, particularly of the poet Igor' Severianin,[19] it is nevertheless reasonably competent, as the following excerpt from a poem about Odessa in April indicates:

Segodnia vozdukh chist i svetel
I pakhnet morem . . . A vdali
Nad gorodom, kad budto veter
Po nebu gonit korabli . . . .

. . . A vecherom, kogda tak yarki
V zelenom nebe fonari,
Vse zolotitsia v golom parke
Ot ugasaiushchei zari. . . .[20]

(Today the air is clean and bright
and it smells of the sea. . . And in the distance
Above the city, it's as though the wind
Is pushing ships across the sky . . .

. . . And in the evening, when the lamps
are so bright in the
green sky,
Everything turns *gold*
in the naked park
From the extinguishing
sunset . . .) (Italics added)

As E. I. Rozanova observes, "These verses breathe the air of Odessa, they are filled with the sun, the sea, and the greenery."[21] In another poem from this cycle called "The Boulevard" (*Bul'var*) Olesha describes the dark blue (*sinii*) color of the pavement on the boulevard.[22] Thus it can be seen that already in the poetry of his teenage years the dominant hues of Odessa for Olesha are associated with the colors blue and green and with the sunlight. Later, in most of his major mature works, such as *Envy, Three Fat Men,* and the short stories, the setting is almost invariably in springtime or in summer. Only a few of Olesha's stories, such as the ones just mentioned, are explicitly set in Odessa. Yet, even in the works such as *Envy,* whose setting is clearly not Odessa, there is an unmistakable Odessan subtext that manifests itself in their sunny landscapes of green and blue. Even after moving to Moscow in 1922, Olesha preserves the perception of landscape he acquired in his youth by setting his works in spring and summer, the time of year when his characteristic greens and blues are richest, just at that time when the northern landscape comes closest to matching its southern counterpart.

Olesha employs spring and summer as the time of action in his works for another important reason: these are the times of year that elicit the feelings of gaiety, holiday, and liberation from the everyday that he so frequently evokes in his work. In Odessa, Olesha took part in a literary circle, "The Green Lamp," a name borrowed from a group Pushkin had been a member of. One of his contemporaries, Boris Bobovich, relates that when the members of "The Green Lamp" earned a little money from the pieces they wrote for a satire magazine called *The Bomb* (*Bomba*), they would go to a certain bar and drink it up in the form of beer. On one of these occasions, Olesha offered the following toast: "To Blok, to poetry, to music, to *spring carnivals* on earth!" (italics added).[23]

For Olesha praise of spring carnivals and flights of fancy into a fantastic, carnival-like world are not simply manifestations of youthful romanticism and exuberance. They are an integral, permanent part of his psychic baggage. No matter how dreary or oppressively mundane his existence becomes, he always keeps a corner of his imagination free for his spring carnivals.

Olesha's capacity for living an inner life outside of everyday reality struck many of those who knew him. For example, Konstantin Paustovsky attests to the fact that Olesha was a lifelong fantast:

> It always seemed to me (and perhaps it was really so) that his whole life Yury Karlovich conversed to himself with geniuses and children, with happy women and kind eccentrics. . . . There existed around Olesha a special life, selected by himself from the reality that surrounded him and embellished by his winged imagination. This life sounded around him like the branch he described in *Envy* that is full of flowers and leaves.
>
> Olesha was continuously in love with life. Reality was illuminated by the reflection of some sort of unique inner holidays.[24]

Vladimir Lidin, another contemporary, writing about a conversation with Olesha, substantially corroborates the notion that Olesha's imagination frequently took him at least one step beyond everyday reality. Olesha once said to Lidin, "Why haven't we drunk a bottle of good wine together? I mean real burgundy. Why don't they sell burgundy here? Balzac described it, it's the wine of the classics. Is it possible we aren't classics yet?"[25]

One of the most important and provocative descriptions of Olesha may be found in Valentin Kataev's *My Diamond Wreath* (*Almaznyi moi venets*) (1981). In this work, which combines fiction with memoirs largely on the model of Olesha's *No Day without a Line,* Kataev refers to himself and Olesha as "eternal friends-rivals, or even enemies who were in love with each other."[26] The name Kataev gives Olesha, "*klyuchik,*" is a diminutive of the Russian word for "key," *klyuch,* that indicates his central role in the book. Olesha is more than a model and a main character in *My Diamond Wreath;* he is the narrator's alter ego. Perhaps a case could even be made that Olesha is a special kind of coauthor, so powerful is his presence. Despite the semifictional nature of *Diamond Wreath* and the tremendously emotional and subjective relationship of its author to Olesha, the book provides substantial confirmation of much of what others found in Olesha, as well as new and valuable information of its own. For example, one of Kataev's anecdotes captures the essence of the creative caprice so many of Olesha's contemporaries saw in him. Once when a chess tournament was being held in Moscow, Olesha told Kataev that the game lacked only one piece for it to be complete: the dragon. Characteristically, to all of Kataev's objections based on reason and the logic of the game, Olesha held fast to his original proposal.[27]

Kataev describes primarily the time he and Olesha spent together from the late teens to the early thirties, when they were virtually inseparable and led an unabashedly Bohemian style of life in which wild whimsy, artistic fancy, and zany escapades reigned supreme. In reading *Diamond Wreath* one is frequently struck by the impression that both Kataev and Olesha lived life as though it were really an ongoing commentary on world literature. Personal experiences were valuable not so much in themselves as they were as material for speculating about how they might be related to something in the works of such writers as Gogol, Mayakovsky, or Hoffmann. Both Kataev and Olesha actively cultivated a sensibility of art as life and life as art. Olesha in particular seems to have been adept at treating and even acting out daily occurrences as though they were actually a familiar fictional event or plot.

In some instances it appears that neither Olesha nor Kataev

fully understood that their love of jocosity and literary prankish-
ness could have serious consequences. This lack of understanding
was evident in a series of incidents involving Olesha's first love, a
girl whose nickname was *"druzhok"* (little friend). According to
Kataev's account, after a long affair of ecstatic infatuation with
Olesha this girl suddenly married another man. Soon, however,
she announced to Kataev and Olesha that she would like to be ab-
ducted from this person, and they were only too happy to oblige.
Subsequently, Olesha once again spirited her away from another
man she was living with. Ultimately, when this new lover
threatened to commit suicide, *druzhok* returned to him. Olesha
continued to meet with the couple socially as though nothing had
changed, but the affair with *druzhok* was over forever.[28]

Kataev believes that the failure of this first love helped to give
Olesha's work its creative spark and eventually led to his self-
destruction.[29] Kataev's interpretation is strongly colored by his
own unrequited love for the writer Mikhail Bulgakov's sister. He
is also greatly influenced by what he sees as the inspirational yet
destructive roles played by failed love affairs in the lives and
works of Mayakovsky and Esenin.[30] The idea that failed or unrequited love can be a stimulus to artistic creation is of course not
original with Kataev. The fact that Olesha nowhere directly addresses questions of his personal love life may indeed indicate that
the subject contained too deep a wound to discuss openly. With
respect to the question of self-destruction, perhaps Kataev over-
looks the possibility that certain personalities seem to find the
means or the excuse to destroy themselves with or without any
outside help. If anything clear emerges from Olesha's muddled
and bizarre first love it is that he himself behaved with great
whimsicality and impracticality. In capriciousness he was out-
done only by his partner.

Olesha's disdain for the everyday is reflected in his writing, his
speech, his thought, and both his early and later life. Even as an
adult he was hopelessly incapable of managing his daily affairs,
and he treated money with contempt. Victor Shklovsky reports
that when Olesha was evacuated from Moscow to Ashkhabad in
Turkistan during World War II, he neglected to continue payment
of his rent. After the war, when he returned to Moscow, his apartment had been given to someone else, and he was forced to
wander about and rent rooms from others.[31]

Once, in better times, he and his wife, Olga Suok-Olesha,

celebrated a personal triumph by walking the streets of Moscow late at night and throwing thirty-ruble notes into the windows of basement apartments.[32] When Olesha had no money, he was not ashamed to borrow it; when he did have money, he did not hesitate to give it away. Olesha's dress also underscored his low regard for the mundane and the conventional. In his later years he cultivated a disheveled appearance by wearing an old, worn-out sportcoat. Yet, in the lapel of that coat he always wore a red rose. When Olesha died, he lay in his coffin with a red rose in his jacket.[33] The rose was an outer physical symbol of the inner world Olesha always carried with him in his imagination.

Olesha's lack of practicality and refusal to deal with the trivial tasks of the here and now, while endearing from a certain point of view, were not without some debilitating consequences. One of the main reasons Olesha did not accomplish more than he did in his career is that he could not manage time. Like many masters of literary short forms, Olesha worked very slowly and with considerable difficulty. Yet, the tremendous number of manuscripts and fragments he left unfinished indicates that he was a chronic procrastinator.[34]

There are other reasons why Olesha did not fulfill all of the expectations both he and others had for himself. Having grown accustomed to group literary activity in his early years in Odessa and subsequently in Moscow, when he worked for the magazine *The Whistle* (*Gudok*), Olesha apparently had difficulty in disciplining himself to spend enough time working alone in his study. Instead, he spent a disproportionate amount of time working at a table in public restaurants, first at a Georgian restaurant opposite the Telegraph Building on Tverskoi Boulevard, now Gorky Street, and later in the Hotel National on the edge of Red Square in Moscow. Invariably Olesha spent most of his time talking with friends and passersby, drinking, and going for walks. He took special delight in social contact with other people and was considered by many to have had excellent acting skills. Within his own circle of friends and acquaintances he was often the center of attention on account of his highly developed wit and his penchant for delivering winged phrases and aphorisms. Olesha was also known for his generosity in suggesting ideas for stories to other writers.[35]

Olesha worked for *The Whistle* between 1922 and 1929 as a writer of satirical verse under the pseudonym of "The Chisel"

(*Zubilo*). These satirical verses were extremely popular—so popular in fact that they have been remembered over the years by some readers, and they even inspired the imitation of at least one "false Chisel." Here is a sample of "The Chisel" at work:

Zria bel'ia ne sobirai, —
Govoriu bez shutki:
V nashei bane popii rai,
A rabochim—dudki![36]

(Don't gather your laundry for nothing, —
I tell you it's no joke.
In our bath it's a priest's paradise,
But the workers can forget it!)

Beyond preparing Olesha for writing a brief one-act play in verse and some children's verse, including cartoons, however, his early work for *The Whistle* has no lasting literary value and is virtually unrelated to his major work in prose.[37] Apart from writing, Olesha would speak before audiences of railway workers—*The Whistle* was the organ of the railway industry—and could do both spontaneous and prepared verse *burimé*, that is, the composition of verses on the basis of rhymes given to him by others.[38]

Most of the writers who were associated with the early years of *The Whistle* have looked back on this period with fondness and nostalgia.[39] One exception was Mikhail Bulgakov, who is reported to have hated his work at the journal.[40] In addition to Olesha and Bulgakov, the writers who contributed to *The Whistle* in the 1920s include Ilia I'lf (Fainzelberg), Valentin Kataev, and Isaac Babel. They are among the best and most important literary figures of the Soviet period. They did some of their work for *The Whistle* collectively and would often gather to exchange humorous tales and anecdotes that would become the basis for their satires and printed stories.[41] In this respect their activities resemble those of the Serapion brothers and other groups of the 1920s who were fond of reading their works aloud to each other and other collective activities. It is possible that interaction with so many stimulating colleagues gave Olesha the impetus he needed to harness his own talent to the composition of fiction of lasting importance. During the period he worked at *The Whistle*, Olesha produced most of his best work, *Envy, Three Fat Men* (*Tri tolstiaka*) (1928), and the stories of the *Cherry Stone* (*Vishnevaia kostochka*) cycle (1929).

Olesha received some of the notoriety he desired as "The Chisel." His fame was further enhanced by the publication of *Envy* in 1927, and to a large degree Olesha's reputation as a writer is still based on this novel. The novel's heavy concentration of vivid imagery and compelling thematics made a tremendous impression that was almost universally favorable. Newspapers from *The Metallurgist* (*Metallist*) to *The Nizhegorod Commune* and journals from *The Whistle* to *The Young Guard* (*Molodaia gvardiia*) proclaimed *Envy* a success and its author a new and powerful talent. *Pravda* announced that "*Envy* puts Olesha forward into the front ranks of writers who stand close to the circles of proletarian artists."[42]

Olesha's reputation as a writer with sound proletarian credentials was short lived, however, and not long after its publication *Envy* became the source of an animated debate that continues even today. As the 1920s drew to a close, the ideological and class battle lines in the Soviet Union began to be drawn more tightly on all fronts, including the literary one. Olesha came to be classified as a fellow traveler from a petty bourgeois background. The debate surrounding *Envy* has centered on the portrayal of its characters, such as Nikolai Kavalerov, Ivan and Andrei Babichev, and Volodya Makarov. One of the reasons the novel had such a great impact is that it describes in compelling terms some of the dilemmas of the intelligentsia in postrevolutionary Russia. V. Pertsov even claims that in its time the novel was the only one of its kind to deal not with the past but with the problems of the present. The appeal of *Envy* is not so much that it solves these problems but that it states them correctly and persuasively.[43] The efforts of Kavalerov and Ivan Babichev to stage a last stand for traditional values of emotional and artistic sensitivity are especially poignant. In the eyes of some critics, however, the quandaries and exploits of Ivan and Kavalerov came to be viewed as frivolous and irrelevant in an era of socialist building.[44]

Over the years, much Soviet criticism has tended to oversimplify *Envy* into little more than a contest between positive and negative characters. Exactly who is positive and who is negative depends partly on the given critic and partly on the given era in which the criticism is made. For example, in describing the up-and-down fate of Andrei Babichev in Soviet criticism, Belinkov says wryly that "Comrade Babichev perished in 1937 as a result of unfounded repression. In 1956 he was completely rehabilitated."[45]

Until recently there has been relatively little detailed investigation of Olesha's distinctive stylistics and poetics in Soviet criticism. For this reason, M. O. Chudakova's book, *The Mastery of Yury Olesha (Masterstvo Yuriia Oleshi)* (1972), is an important milestone in the critical literature on Olesha because it is the first work to undertake a penetrating and thorough examination of Olesha's stylistics. Some of the reaction to Chudakova's book has served to underscore how well entrenched the ideological and quasi-sociological approaches to Olesha are. Pertsov, for example, finds Chudakova's study one-sided and is unwilling to grant that she goes beyond the analysis of Olesha's artistic devices in order to reveal his view of the world.[46] Even Belinkov, whose stated purpose is to overthrow the conventional criticism on Olesha, concentrates his attack on the ideological aspects of Olesha's characters but introduces no new methodology.

Perhaps the greatest myth surrounding Olesha is the idea that he went through a long period of silence. Shklovsky is one of the critics who has helped to cultivate that myth.[47] One thing Belinkov has demonstrated conclusively is that the period 1935–60, the time usually designated as Olesha's silent interval, was in fact a time of great activity. The total volume of material produced by Olesha then was greater than in the period immediately preceding it, the period that is usually considered his most productive.[48]

In order to form a truer conception of the nature of Olesha's supposed silence it is instructive to examine briefly what exactly he did during this time. One reason it is possible to state that the total number of items published by Olesha actually increases rather than decreases is that he published a large number of newspaper and journal articles on a variety of subjects. Some of these, such as "On Election Day" (*V den' vyborov*) (1937), are extremely short,[49] and Olesha wrote everything from movie reviews to articles for the sports page. He did not cease writing fiction, however, and published a number of sketches and short stories in the late thirties and early forties. It was at this time that Olesha became increasingly involved with the cinema, and he spent a great deal of his time writing the scenarios for *Swamp Soldiers (Bolotnye soldaty)* (1938), *Engineer Kochin's Mistake (Oshibka inzhenera Kochina)* (1939), and *The Little Lieutenant (Malen'kii leitenant*) (1942). Even his period of evacuation to Turkistan resulted in a number of stories, including "The Turkoman" (*Turkmen*) (1944) and "The Mirror" (*Zerkal'tse*) (1945). Nor did Olesha cease publishing in the late 1940s.

If there is a period of his career that resembles a hiatus during which he was unable to write, then perhaps it is the early 1950s. During this time most of Olesha's published work consists of reviews of other people's stories in *Literaturnaia gazeta*.[50] In the latter half of the 1950s Olesha writes scenarios of classic works, such as Dostoevsky's *Idiot* (1958), and children's cartoons, such as "A Little Girl at the Circus" (1958).

Silence as it relates to Olesha has to do with the silence of literary critics about his work and not with any lack of activity on his part. The plain fact is that most of Olesha's fiction, sketches, and drama written after the middle of the 1930s is not on a level with his work of the twenties and early thirties and therefore has not received nearly as much attention. The reasons for this will be dealt with in the following chapters.

During the last years of his life, Olesha came to be increasingly aware of the fact that he had accomplished in literature a great deal less than he might have done. He was actually rather touchy on the subject of his literary output. An exchange between Olesha and another writer who had been successful in publishing large volumes of his work illustrates not only Olesha's sensitivity to the question of his creative productivity but also his razor-sharp tongue.

> SUCCESSFUL WRITER: You haven't published very much during your whole lifetime, Yury Karlovich. I could read it all in one night.
>
> OLESHA: And in one night I could write everything that you have written in your lifetime.[51]

Prompted by a sense of his advancing age and the desire to make up for lost time, Olesha worked intensely during the last years of his life, adding a great deal of material to his already large body of notes. He made a return to "big literature" in 1956 with the publication of some brief excerpts from these notes. After his death in 1960, his notes appeared in several journals in 1961 and 1963. Finally, in 1965 his notes were published in the form of an independent book as *No Day without a Line*. This book gave Olesha a third and posthumous period of fame. Even the 1974 edition of *No Day without a Line*, which contains several passages not included in 1965, does not include all of the large amount of material available.[52] Although Olesha is, of course, the author of *No Day without a Line*, the book's final form is the product of a kind of collective authorship. After his death a team of scholars, which included at different times Viktor Shklovsky, Belinkov, and Mikhail Gromov, assembled his notes and sketches in collaboration with his widow, Olga Suok-Olesha, into a whole book. As Shklovsky recalls: "We sorted by kinds of paper, by the typewriters, by the yellowness of the papers. We found plans. And there lay a book ready on the table; it had taken shape in a briefcase and then in a book."[53]

Olesha's life and works are intimately bound up with the popular culture of his time. As Shklovsky so aptly puts it, "The world of Olesha is the world of sport and the circus."[54] Olesha indicates in an autobiographical sketch published after his death that part of his attraction for Europe has to do with the fact that sport and the new technology first developed there. "The thought of Europe agitated my imagination tremendously. In Europe in that epoch aviation was beginning and sport was beginning. In Europe technology had blossomed. There fairy-tale automobile races took place, there stood the Eiffel Tower. And then Wells fell into my hands. I know that the summer coloration of *Envy* is from Wells, it is from a dream about Europe, from the pictures of aviation and sport which appeared in my imagination then."[55]

This description of the influence of H. G. Wells on the summer colors of *Envy* would appear to contradict the assertion made above that the novel's landscape derives largely from Odessa. Actually, there is no contradiction here, for in Olesha's mind, "it seemed that Odessa was more closely tied to Europe than to Russia."[56] Thoughts of Wells and dreams of Europe serve to highlight, rather than obscure, the summery Odessan character of Olesha's landscapes.

Olesha's fascination with the products of technology, particularly the mobile ones, such as the bicycle, motorcycle, automobile, and airplane, manifests itself from *Envy* through *No Day without a Line*. But as Olesha writes in *No Day without a Line*, it is the circus that attracted him most of all. "The circus is the basis of my life" (409). He explains what the circus means to him:

As a boy and for many years later already as an adult, of all the spectacles I loved the circus the most.

Yes, and it wasn't only as a spectacle that I perceived the circus. No, my relationship to it was more complex, with me thoughts of glory were intertwined with the circus. I imagined to myself that I would be a famous circus performer, an acrobat! And an emerging sensibility found its secret embodiment in the images of the circus. (408)

Olesha believes that his childhood dream to be able to do a somersault, one of the circus's most characteristic acts, is tied in some way with the first stirrings in himself of the future artist; this dream is an indication that he would move "in the direction of the creation of the new, the unusual, in the direction of brightness and beauty" (409). As the course of his career demonstrates, the images of the circus are connected not just with the first awakening of his artistic creativity but also with the specific imagery of his works and their whole poetic makeup.

One of the most enduring and the most significant of Olesha's interests in popular culture is his lifelong preoccupation and involvement with sport, particularly soccer. Olesha is one of the most important observers of early Russian soccer, which has been the most popular sport in Russia since about 1910.[57] As he writes in *No Day without a Line*, "I saw the dawn of Russian soccer" (412). He was also proud of the fact that he was the first important Soviet Russian writer to introduce the theme of sport into fiction.[58] The description of the soccer match in *Envy* is the first of its kind in Soviet Russian literature. One of its only predecessors, if not the only predecessor in Russian literature, is Tolstoy's description of the steeplechase in *Anna Karenina*, where Vronsky accidentally breaks the back of his horse, Frou Frou.

For Olesha sport was not simply a childhood infatuation; it was a love of a lifetime. In his later years he wrote articles for the sports pages on important international matches held in Moscow.[59] He also attended soccer matches, often with his friend Andrei Starostin. What Olesha saw in the playing and watching of sport was the same kind of phenomenon he found in watching the circus. What he intuitively sought in sport and in the circus was a life outside of the usual rut, a life with a different set of rules than those of the everyday. Sport and the circus are among the few forms of contemporary life that have historic and symbolic ties with the life of the carnival.

Modern sport, the birth of which Olesha witnessed, has its origins in folk games that were played as part of carnival celebrations in early modern Europe.[60] The circus also has its roots in the life of the carnival, where costumes and eccentric behavior take the place of the quotidian. It is just this spirit of the carnival in sport and the circus that draws Olesha to them.

Olesha's poetics form a rich, diverse, and complex system in which several elements interact with each other. Nevertheless, it is possible to discern both a definite hierarchy in his poetical system and a set of principles that governs it. The three dominant elements in this hierarchy are estrangement, carnival, and dialogue. The unifying impulse behind these diverse elements is his persistent need to do and to take things out of their usual course and to work in opposition to accepted practices and conventions. While working against traditional norms, however, Olesha retains a distinctive knack for seeing both sides of an issue or question[61] and thereby gives his work a distinctly dialogical quality.

Because the Soviet critic Mikhail Bakhtin is the chief exponent of carnival and dialogue as terms of literary criticism, and because so much of the critical apparatus of this work is either based directly on or derived from Bakhtin, it is appropriate to indicate briefly why his critical theories are so poignantly relevant to an examination of Olesha.

Bakhtin's wide-ranging work has achieved a considerable reputation and influence in a number of fields, especially in literary and linguistic studies, anthropology, and philosophy.[62] In fact, it is no exaggeration to say that Bakhtin may be regarded as one of the most important thinkers of the twentieth century. This being the case, there is the obvious danger that his theories will be applied too widely in various scholarly fields of inquiry. On the other hand, Bakhtin's analysis of how human beings communicate is compelling precisely because it is conceived in universal terms. Therefore, it is not surprising that his ideas should find currency in a number of different areas. With specific regard to Olesha, it is clear that Bakhtin's notions of carnival and dialogue are particularly apt for elucidating these central features of Olesha's work.

At first glance there would appear to be little in common between the sometimes libertine, liquor-drinking Olesha and the ascetic, tea-drinking Bakhtin.[63] Although Bakhtin is known for his participation in various circles, especially with Pavel Medvedev and Valentin Voloshinov, he was for large parts of his life something of a recluse.[64] Olesha, on the other hand, was compulsively gregarious. Where Bakhtin is intellectual, analytical, and scholarly, Olesha is intuitive, spontaneous, and artistic. Nevertheless, there are some important points of contact and even coincidence between the two. Not the least of these is the fact that they both spent a significant portion of their formative years in Odessa, where they lived for most of the 1910s. There is no evidence that the two ever met, but it is not inconceivable that they might have crossed paths at some point (Bakhtin was only four years older than Olesha), given the fashion popular in most intellectual and artistic circles of that time of meeting frequently in groups and staging various kinds of public spectacles.

In describing the importance of Odessa in the formation of Bakhtin's world view, Katerina Clark and Michael Holquist have noted that the spirit of "fun and irreverence" typical of the city made it "an appropriate setting for a chapter in the life of a man who was to become the philosopher of heteroglossia and carnival."[65]

Odessa was exactly the sort of place to engender a sense of carnival in its inhabitants. As a seaport, Odessa was a polyglot society, even if many of those who made it so were only transients. It was also a seaport with a well-developed high culture that produced not only Babel, Kataev, and Il'f and Petrov, but also the likes of Heifetz and Horowitz. At the same time Odessa was home to an equally well-developed underworld culture that has been immortalized in Babel's portrait of Benya Krik and his cohorts. This coexistence and intermingling of radically contrasting cultural and social planes was in fact one of the cardinal features of the carnival. If the special cultural mix of Odessa could have helped to inspire the leading scholar of carnival, it might also have been instrumental in stimulating an artist of the carnival such as Olesha.

With its great cultural diversity, it is little wonder that Odessa should have engendered scholars and writers whose creative output is bound up with popular culture. Here then is perhaps the most important connection between Olesha and Bakhtin. For each was fascinated by the popular culture not just of Odessa and

Russia but of Europe on the whole. Bakhtin's involvement with popular culture is unquestionably more profound and more deeply grounded in history than Olesha's. Yet, Olesha stands out among his contemporaries for his keen feeling for the popular culture of his day. Olesha comes to a carnivalistic sensibility through his love of such folk forms as sport and the circus indirectly, intuitively, and largely unconsciously. Bakhtin's apprehension of the carnival is more analytical and calculated and certainly much more thoroughly worked out.

According to Bahktin, the carnival is essentially an expression of a popular counterculture which demonstratively sets itself in opposition to the official culture of church and state. The carnival and a carnivalistic mentality are attractive to both Bakhtin and Olesha because each of them was opposed to established canons.[66] Each seems instinctively to have rebelled against everything that was conventionalized and canonized. As Clark and Holquist have written of Bakhtin, "He speaks of the 'renewal of old objects by a new use or new and unexpected juxtapositions,' of the importance of destroying the old images of things and looking at them anew."[67]

One of the many anomalies associated with Bakhtin is the fact that although his lifelong battle against the canonical appears to ally him with the avant-garde, he was not interested in the avant-garde writing that was being done all around him.[68] Contrary to what one might expect, there is a singular point of concurrence between Bahktin and a conscious avant-gardist such as Viktor Shklovsky, with whom he was at odds on most issues. We can now see with the benefit of hindsight that Bakhtin's penchant for renewing our perception of old objects dovetails exactly with the poetics of avant-gardists like Shklovsky, who deliberately grounded their work on the same principle. Perhaps the resolution to this paradoxical concurrence has to do with the fact that from the conventional point of view the carnival is society or social life that has been made unfamiliar.

Olesha too was intent on tearing down the old and replacing it with new forms and possibilities. One of the principal ways in which he does this is through estrangement or "defamiliarization."[69] Defamiliarization in Olesha involves not only the technique of creating imagery that makes the reader see the world from fresh or novel points of view. Defamiliarization is a force that embraces far more than imagery alone; it motivates the very process by which Olesha composes the forms and structures of which his works consist. Indeed, he is a writer who can be said to have fundamentally affected the ways in which readers perceive whole generic systems. In treading along and across what Gary Saul Morson calls the thresholds and boundaries of genres, Olesha continually makes the reader reevaluate and recode the structures of his works in unfamiliar ways.[70]

Olesha's attraction to the carnival is a logical outgrowth of his penchant for avoiding the usual and for battling convention. Carnival is meant here primarily in the sense that it is defined by Bakhtin in his works on Rabelais and Dostoevsky. In Bakhtin's analysis elements of the historical phenomenon of the carnival have penetrated certain literary forms and works, making them in effect carnivalized or carnivalistic.[71]

Olesha's works do not uniformly display the features of the carnival as described by Bakhtin. Nevertheless, the carnival is a powerful force in several of Olesha's best and most important works. Not only do these works portray the world as out of its usual rut, or in a state where the normal rules of conduct have been suspended—sometimes to be replaced by a new set of rules—but they also frequently exhibit the specific imagery of the carnival.

In Bakhtin's conception of dialogue the narrative structure of fiction may be characterized by an intense competition among a number of voices with different social, linguistic, or emotional orientations. For Bakhtin the word in a literary text is not simply monological, that is, addressed to itself, but it is dialogical, that is, directed to the word of the listener-reader. Put another way, each word does not exist somehow independently on its own; rather it anticipates and actively interacts with the word of another. It is central to Bakhtin's conception of dialogue that there can be no final or finalizing word in a true dialogue. On another level, Bakhtin also conceives of dialogue as the active juxtaposition of a work's structual elements.[72] Olesha's poetics are so thoroughly dialogical in the Bakhtinian sense, because he constantly and ubiquitously places themes, motifs, characters, and especially narrative voices in a dynamic competition with each other that is never fully resolved.

1 /
From Metafiction to Metaliterature

Ancestors and Models

In the fifth letter of his book *Zoo, or Letters Not about Love* (*Zoo, ili pis'ma ne o liubvi*) (1924), Viktor Shklovsky writes:

> Our business is the creation of new things. At the moment, Remizov wants to create a book with no plot, with no "man's fate" lodged at the base of the composition. He's writing one book made from bits and pieces—that's *Russia in Writ*, a book made from scraps of books; he's writing another one built on Rozanov's letters.
>
> It's impossible to write a book in the old way. Bely knows that, Rozanov knew it well.[1]

Throughout most of his career Yury Olesha wrote as though he too had made it his business to create "new things." In so doing he was participating in a process that takes place in all eras but which became particularly acute and dynamic in the second and third decades of this century in Russian letters. At that time writers such as Rozanov, Remizov, Bely, Shklovsky himself, Boris Pil'niak, and Zamiatin all undertook in various ways to rewrite the rules by which literary prose in general and fiction in particular are constructed. Although he was a relative latecomer to this endeavor, Olesha made an important contribution to it.

Shklovsky's use of the word "new" should not, of course, be taken in an absolute sense but rather programmatically, because new forms and new genres do not simply spring into existence independently of what has come before them. The development of genres is obviously a complex process. Genres flourish, fade out of view, and reemerge. They may recombine with other genres to produce synthetic genres or hybrid types. Something like this process takes place in Tolstoy's *War and Peace*, which synthesizes into a single, coherent structure elements of the family chronicle, the historical novel, and even the nonfictional form of the philosophical essay.[2]

Shklovsky's dicta about new books versus old books are a shorthand way of saying that in the era following the nineteenth century in Russian literature writers must find forms that distinguish themselves from the generic models that had already become frozen as classics. His choice of Vasily Rozanov as an inspiration for new directions is no coincidence, for Rozanov made a seminal contribution to the development of genre in the twentieth century with his books *A Secluded Place (Uedinennoe)* (1912), *Fallen Leaves (Opavshie list'ia)* (1913), and *The Apocalypse of Our Time (Apokalipsis nashego vremeni)* (1917–18). Rozanov's innovation, just as Shklovsky indicates, is to compose his works by compiling various fragments to form a single book. As we will see subsequently, this technique already had a forerunner in Dostoevsky's *Diary of a Writer (Dnevnik pisatelia)* (1874–81). Rozanov's consistent implementation of composition by fragments became a model for writers such as Alexei Remizov, Boris Pil'niak, and, of course, Shklovsky.

As Gary Saul Morson has observed, "The central argument of *Zoo* is that the processes of structuring and inferring structure from literary works have become automatized."[3] To remedy this situation Shklovsky does several things. First he constantly bares the devices he employs in the composition of *Zoo*. For example, he often prefaces the letters of *Zoo* with not only a summary of what they contain but also a description of how he will communicate that information. At the same time Shklovsky reframes the constituent parts of his book so that they will be perceived outside of the context in which they might normally appear. For instance, he combines letters of his own invention with real letters that a woman has sent him. In this way he assumes authority over her letters so that he now becomes their author and they acquire a new semiotic status in the structure of his book.[4]

Shklovsky's technique is analogous to the practice in so-called pop art of taking real objects, such as junkyard relics, and reframing them in the setting of an art gallery. In this process the artist becomes a collector and framer, and the viewer now perceives an artistic structure in the items the artist has collected. The net effect of Shklovsky's approach is to make the reader rethink devices and structures that have become familiar and even to reconsider the ways in which we read whole genres.

In much the same way that Shklovsky lifts real letters from their original context and reframes them within the structure of

Zoo, Boris Pil'niak incorporates various bureaucratic, military, and historical documents into the texts of his novels and thereby becomes their framer or author. Pil'niak's most extravagant implementation of this device is the insertion of a copy of a newspaper into the binding of his novel *The Volga Flows into the Caspian Sea* (*Volga vpadaet v kaspiiskoe more*) (1930). In this and other novels such as *The Naked Year* (*Golyi god*) (1920) and *Machines and Wolves* (*Mashiny i volki*) (1922), certain documents may actually act to carry forward the plot line. In this way Pil'niak greatly increases both the difficulty and the strangeness of his narrative. Consequently, he defamiliarizes the very conventions that readers have generally employed to understand novelistic plot.[5]

Evgeny Zamiatin also employs documents in his novel *We* (*My*) (1924). Whereas Pil'niak freely mixes genuine documents with some of his own invention, Zamiatin relies primarily on documents he has made up himself. Nevertheless, they too may increase the degree of difficulty experienced by the reader in decoding the novel's structure. Zamiatin, like Shklovsky, specializes in baring the devices of his work to induce the reader to see its structure in novel and unexpected ways. Zamiatin constantly addresses the reader, breaks the illusion of reality, and freely discourses on the process of writing the novel. All of these techniques underscore the fact that *We* is "a novel about the birth of the novel, literature about literature's rediscovery."[6]

The techniques of writers such as Rozanov, Shklovsky, Pil'niak, and Zamiatin have important consequences for our understanding of the lines that have traditionally distinguished genres from one another. A compilation of fragments can now be given a plot so that it tells a story in the manner of a novel. A novel, on the other hand, can now be written without a plot. What is ostensibly nonfiction may employ the devices of fiction so that the reader has to decide for himself whether it may not be a special kind of fiction. Also, nonfictional material from the everyday world may acquire fictional properties if it is reframed in the structure of a work of fiction. Genres can coexist and even compete with each other within the framework of a single book. To borrow Morson's terms again, the author may doubly encode a work so that the reader has to work out for himself what its genre is.[7] This is exactly the process that takes place in so many of Olesha's works, where heterogeneous genres and elements are in competition with each other and where the reader has constantly to discover and rediscover the rules of structure and genre.

The Many Texts of *Three Fat Men*

Three Fat Men (*Tri tolstiaka*) (1928) occupies a special place in Olesha's work for a number of reasons. It is the one work, more so even than *Envy*, by which Olesha's name is best known in the Soviet Union, because *Three Fat Men*, originally published as a novel, has also been made into a play, an opera, a ballet, a film, a puppet show, and a radio drama.[8] Moreover, the extraordinary multitextuality of *Three Fat Men* is by no means limited to its external forms. Within the bounds of the original prose novel one may discern a number of distinct genres. Olesha himself calls the book an adventure novel in "In the World" (*V mire*) (1930) (234), but it is an adventure novel written for children, so that the reader may find in it a modern children's story. Some have viewed it as closest to the folktale. Shklovsky, ever alert to new generic possibilities, reads *Three Fat Men* as the first revolutionary fairy tale for children in Soviet literature. In addition to these many texts, *Three Fat Men* contains a remarkable complex of disparate material, including significant echoes of Shakespeare and passages that clearly derive from the slapstick comedy of the cinema.

Naturally, we have to take seriously Olesha's own reading of *Three Fat Men* as an adventure novel because it prominently displays the major characteristics of the genre: exotic setting and characters and a great deal of action and intrigue. *Three Fat Men* is set in some unspecified time and unnamed foreign land. Shklovsky sees in the novel's setting an echo of Olesha's Polish heritage and believes that *Three Fat Men* takes place in a medieval Polish town. Pertsov, on the other hand, thinks that the details of clothing and custom indicate that it takes place sometime in the late eighteenth century.[9] This discrepancy is not an indication of failure on Olesha's part but rather a testimony to his success in producing just the sort of generalized, nonspecific impression of other times and other places that is crucial to an adventure novel. There are also features of the setting in *Three Fat Men* that come straight from Olesha's imagination, and these too contribute to an overall aura of exoticism. The description of the center of town is the most prominent example of this.

They called this square Star Square for the following reason. It was surrounded by enormous houses of the same height and shape and was covered by a glass cupola that made it look like a colossal circus. In the center of the cupola, at a terrible height shone the largest lantern in the world. It was a sphere of surprising size. Enclosed by an iron ring, and hanging on powerful cables, it brought to mind the planet Saturn. Its color was so beautiful and so unlike any other earthly color that the people gave this lantern the marvelous name of Star. Thus they began to call the whole square. (105)

Olesha further enhances the exotic flavor of *Three Fat Men* by giving his characters foreign-sounding names. Some of these names do not have an immediately obvious origin, but they are clearly not Russian: Tub, Tibul the tightrope walker, and Suok the heroine, who also works in the circus. This last name is, incidentally, the maiden name of Olesha's wife, Olga Gustafovna Suok, and is of Austrian origin.[10] It also appears that the circus that visited Odessa in Olesha's youth serves as an inspiration for the characters' names. In the Efimov circus that performed in Odessa there were clowns called Tanti and Rosetti.[11] In *Three Fat Men* the name of the heir to the three fat men is Tutti. Other Italian names are Arneri and Prospero, the gunsmith and leader of the rebels. Prospero's name comes from Shakespeare's *The Tempest* and will be discussed in due course.

In his use of foreign names and a generalized foreign setting, Olesha is doubtless indebted to his contemporary Russian writer Alexander Grin.[12] Olesha held Grin's works in great esteem, and in *No Day without a Line* he expresses the belief that Grin has gone undervalued as a writer. Olesha would place Grin on as high a level as Edgar Allan Poe.[13] One of the most striking features of Grin's stories is his employment of non-Russian names, often with an English sound, and unnamed foreign settings that give his works an exotic and sometimes mysterious quality. It is just this quality of exoticism and mystery that Olesha is striving for in his adaptation of Grin's techniques in *Three Fat Men*.

One other complicating factor should be noted in connection with the setting of *Three Fat Men:* the presence of a discernible Odessan undercurrent in Olesha's depiction of the novel's weather and natural colors. The green, summery quality of the landscape in *Three Fat Men* is just like the one found in such works as "In the World" and *No Day without a Line*, which are actually set in Odessa. One of the constant features of Olesha's works is that wherever they are set, in Moscow or even in an unnamed foreign country, Olesha always manages to interject elements of his native Odessa. As will be shown, Olesha's distinctive landscape and setting are important aspects of the carnivalistic ambience characteristic of *Three Fat Men* and many of his other works.

In addition to an exotic setting and characters, an adventure novel requires lots of action and suspense. *Three Fat Men* stands out among Olesha's works, which are generally static with respect to action, as by far the most lively. Characters are pursued, they get away, they are captured, and then finally they escape or are rescued. The two opposing forces in *Three Fat Men*, the troops of the fat men and the revolutionary forces, constantly skirmish with each other. All of this swashbuckling comes to a climax in the rescue of Suok from the three fat men just before she is about to be executed. Olesha knew the components of adventure novels well from his extensive reading of Western fiction,[14] and he uses this rescue scene, which is obligatory in any adventure story, to maximum effect. Even though melodramatic action is almost entirely foreign to his adult fiction, Olesha employs it here with considerable skill and thereby reveals a versatility that is never fully realized in his later work.

Olesha's narrative techniques in *Three Fat Men* are calculated to enhance the suspense and intrigue of the novel to the highest degree possible. For example, when Suok has been caught the narrator says:

> What happened to the doll who had been exposed is unknown. In addition we will for the time being restrain ourselves from other such explanations, specifically, what sort of parrot was sitting in the tree and why the respected zoologist was frightened . . . how the gunsmith Prospero wound up in freedom and where the panther came from; how Suok turned up on the shoulder of the gunsmith. . . .
>
> Everything will become clear in its time. I assure you that no miracles took place and that everything happened, as scientists say, according to the iron laws of logic. (173)

In this passage Olesha summarizes the main points of intrigue and whets the reader's appetite for discovering how they are all resolved. He also exploits his promised exposé of the novel's seemingly mysterious and fantastic occurrences in order to heighten the suspense. Subsequently, the narrator further raises the level of suspense by recapitulating what he and the reader already know about the outcome of the various puzzles. Still later, the narrator bids the reader listen if he is interested in learning more about what happened.

These different asides and apostrophes to the reader have a number of important functions. Most obviously, they act to heighten the reader's interest in the eventual outcome of the action. They also establish an intimate relationship between the narrator and the reader. Such an intimate narrative stance, although operating in a different context with different functions, is to become the dominant one in Olesha's short stories and sketches. Eventually, Olesha's narrative persona reaches a position where he is one-on-one with the reader. In *Three Fat Men* Olesha demonstrates a mastery of just the kind of narrative devices that are needed to establish rapport and confidence with the young reader as well as to make the plot highly suspenseful. Olesha's asides and apostrophes are also part of his technique of baring the devices of which adventure novels, and his in particular, are comprised. Implicit in this is an ongoing discussion of how one writes adventure novels for children.

The resemblance of *Three Fat Men* to Russian folktales, or *skazki*, has already been noted by Aimée and Donald Anderson in the Afterword to the novel's English translation.[15] The book is filled with action, and the treatment of character is not unlike that of a *skazka*, in which characters are shown in either a wholly positive or a wholly negative light with little or no development. According to the Andersons, fantasy in *Three Fat Men* is "limited to the extent to which a group of people can perceive it."[16] This is true for the most part, since many of the motifs and occurrences of *Three Fat Men* that have a fantastic appearance are given a realistic exposé or rationalization by the author. For example, in several parts of the novel it appears that the young circus performer, Suok, and the doll of the heir to the three fat men, Tutti, are fantastically transformed into one another. In every case, however, it turns out to be only an illusion. Another fantastic transformation characteristic of folktales, that of man into animal, seems to take place when the gunsmith, Prospero, is described as dying in the captivity of the three fat men's cage. Ultimately, however, the reader learns that it was not Prospero at all but a man called Tub who has taken on the appearance of a hairy animal. Fantastic events receive no realistic justification in genuine folktales, where unfettered fantasy is prevalent. In *Three Fat Men*, on the other hand, Olesha explains most of the seemingly fantastic events in realistic terms. He underlines the non-miraculous character of the novel by repeating the refrain "There are no miracles" in several places.

Nevertheless, certain events take place in *Three Fat Men* that are never given a complete exposé. A man who sells balloons is transported by a great gust of wind to the palace of the three fat men. There he makes his escape through the bottom of a large saucepan into a secret tunnel. Eventually, he winds up with his head in a cabbage patch. The saucepan is also used by Prospero to make his getaway from the three fat men. In the cases of the balloon vendor and the fantastic saucepan, Olesha never provides a rationalization. In this way he effectively captures the spirit of fantasy that permeates both genuine folktales and much of modern children's literature.

Many individual motifs in *Three Fat Men* enhance its status as a kind of modern folktale. When the dance instructor, Onetwo-threes (*Razdvatris*),[17] is sent away from the palace of the three fat men, he is placed on his horse backwards. The motif of riding backwards on a horse is frequently encountered in Russian folktales about the peasant lad, foolish Ivan (*Ivanushka durachok*). Indeed, Olesha's purpose in his description of Onetwo-threes is to make him appear as foolish as possible.

The kinds of potions with magical properties that are found in the folktales of many nations also play a role in *Three Fat Men*. Doctor Gaspar Arneri uses such a potion to change the color of the skin of Tibul, the tightrope walker, from white to black and back to white again. The purpose of making Tibul look like a "North American Negro" is to help him escape the henchmen of the three fat men, who are trying to capture him, since he is one of the leaders of the revolutionary forces. The three fat men have a potion of their own. Their henchmen place a sleeping potion in the ear of their heir, Tutti, so that he will sleep through the planned execution of Suok, who is to be punished for helping

Prospero escape from their grasp. In both cases Olesha relies on the reader's sense of fantasy rather than a knowledge of medicine to understand the power of these potions.

Revelations of true identity are a common feature of both folktales and adventure novels that figure in *Three Fat Men*. The three fat men do not have a natural heir for themselves so they have kidnaped the young boy Tutti and designated him as their heir. Despite their efforts to instill cruelty in him by exposing him to the cruelty of predatory animals, Tutti remains a mild-mannered young boy. His affection for his doll is a symbol of his kind disposition. At the end of the novel it is revealed that Suok and Tutti are really brother and sister. After the three fat men stole the two from their parents, they gave Suok away to a circus. They kept the boy and had a doll made to look exactly like his sister. Thus is resolved the paradox that a kind boy has endured unharmed the hostile surroundings created by evil men. The motif of a good, kind child held in captivity by evil adults is of course another common theme in folktales, particularly in those collected by the Brothers Grimm.[18]

In several passages of *Three Fat Men* Olesha makes direct references to well-known folktale motifs or folktales themselves. He specifically mentions the transformations of princess into frog and frog into princess that are often found in folktales as a way of introducing his own apparent transformations of Suok into a doll and vice versa (148). Here the reference to the frog and the princess is a means of exposing the device and thereby calling attention to the fact that the author is indeed exploiting the traditions of the genre of folktales. Olesha achieves a similar result in another place where he mentions the three pigs whose place will be taken by a wolf (121). These direct references to folktales and folktale motifs form part of the literary subtext in *Three Fat Men* in which Olesha is conversing with the adult reader and demonstrating to him or her that he is very much aware of the devices and the materials with which he is constructing his own story, that he is in complete control of them, and that he will use them exactly as he sees fit.

Three Fat Men is a pastiche not only of different genres but also of literary allusions. One of the most important of these is found in its relationship to Shakespeare's play *The Tempest* that is signaled by the name of the gunsmith, Prospero. As Robert Szulkin has pointed out, the name Prospero undoubtedly comes from Shakespeare's *The Tempest,* where Prospero is a magician. The principal affinity between *The Tempest* and *Three Fat Men* is that both works are about revolution and power.[19] Although Olesha's Prospero is not endowed with magical powers, it appears near the end of the novel that he has undergone a magical transformation from man into animal. However, this apparently fantastic transformation turns out to be an illusion. In *Three Fat Men* Dr. Arneri, who has potions for changing the color of the characters' skin, is the closest character to a magician in the novel.[20] The changes in identity that take place in *Three Fat Men* form another important link with *The Tempest.* In Shakespeare's play the plot is resolved when Prospero reveals his real identity. Olesha's revelation of Suok's and Tutti's true identities in *Three Fat Men* is an integral part of the story's ultimate resolution.

Olesha's borrowing and recasting aspects of *The Tempest* in *Three Fat Men* create a level of discourse with the adult reader that is usually inaccessible to the child reader. Such a technique is, of course, characteristic of most sophisticated children's literature, such as Lewis Carroll's *Alice in Wonderland* and *Through the Looking Glass.* Here it also epitomizes the extraordinary number of levels on which Olesha addresses his various readers. It should also be pointed out that the presence of a Shakespearean element in *Three Fat Men* underlines the fact that Olesha's apprehension of revolution in the novel is based far more on literary archetypes and motifs than it is on politics.

Olesha was one of the first Russian writers to incorporate techniques and devices from the cinema into his fiction. By so doing in *Three Fat Men* he adds a multimedia aspect to a work that already goes beyond the usual genre boundaries. In reading *Three Fat Men* one can not help but notice that the hilarity and nonsensical absurdity of certain passages has the perceptible flavor of cinematic slapstick comedy. In one scene a guardsman of the three fat men has a pen stick to his rear end. In another passage one of the clowns of the three fat men has his mouth pasted shut by a flat cake. The culmination of the slapstick comedy scenes in *Three Fat Men* takes place when Prospero is escaping and he takes over the confectionery, where sweets and desserts are prepared for the satisfaction of the three fat men's gluttony:

> He turned over jars, and threw around frying pans, funnels, plates, and dishes. Glass flew in all directions and broke with a

crash and a bang; spilled flour swirled in a column, like a simoom in the Sahara; a whirlwind of almonds, raisins, and cherries rose up; sugary sand pelted from the shelves with the roar of a waterfall; a flood of syrups rose to a full three feet; water splashed, fruit rolled, and the copper towers of saucepans gave way. Everything was turned upside down. That's the way it is sometimes in a dream when you are dreaming a dream and you know that it is a dream and therefore you can do anything you like. (172)

The sheer exuberance and playfulness of this scene willy-nilly brings to mind the hilarity of the early silent films, yet it has no match in the rest of Olesha's work. Among Olesha's contemporaries Mikhail Bulgakov is best known for such descriptions of unrestrained pandemonium. Bulgakov's description of Korotkov's destruction of the billiard room in his story "Diaboliad" (D'iavoliada) (1925) is one of his most extravagant in this vein. Bulgakov makes explicit the influence of the cinema that is only implicit in Olesha's *Three Fat Men*. Bulgakov does it by naming the chapter that contains the destruction of the poolroom by Korotkov "A Cinema Chase and the Abyss" (*Parforsnoe kino i bezdna*).[21] Bulgakov revels in this sort of description and returns to it dramatically in *The Master and Margarita*, especially in chapter 27, which is called "The End of Apartment No. 50" (*Konets Kvartiry* No. 50), where Begemot and Koroviev battle the local police. For Olesha, on the other hand, the description of the destruction of the three fat men's confectionery in *Three Fat Men* was an isolated occurrence but an important one for producing the comic action of a children's adventure novel.

Three Fat Men was written during an extremely dynamic and fertile period in Russian children's literature. At this time Kornei Chukovsky, Samuil Marshak, and Daniil Kharms were among the gifted writers who were producing a substantial body of original children's literature in Russian. Eventually, Chukovsky, Marshak, and others also came to translate nearly all of the English nursery rhymes into Russian. Chukovsky and Kharms were especially clever in their use of humorous absurdities and non sequiturs in their children's stories and verses.

To a large extent, however, Olesha operates in *Three Fat Men* outside of the poetic system that Chukovsky and Marshak were helping to create in Russian children's literature in the 1920s. Aside from the eccentric character of Dr. Arneri in *Three Fat Men* that is reminiscent of Dr. Dolittle (especially in Olesha's dramatization of *Three Fat Men*) and the occasional use of non sequiturs, there are few points of contact between Olesha and Chukovsky or the other major children's writers. Olesha's comic techniques are more closely related to cinematic slapstick than they are to the muddles and mix-ups (*perevertyshi*) of Chukovsky and Marshak. Nor does Olesha have much in common with the so-called leftist pedologists, who wanted to inculcate moral and ideological values in a sober and didactic fashion.[22] *Three Fat Men*, to be sure, contains a statement in favor of revolution, but it is a statement that is made not didactically; rather it is made with a light, sometimes even silly touch.

None of these observations should be construed to mean that *Three Fat Men* does not have a discernible relationship with children's literature on the whole. The questions of defining children's literature and determining how it becomes considered so are really quite complex. For the sake of simplicity and the current discussion, let us assume that there are at least three types of good children's literature. A first is that which is intended for children only. Beatrice Potter's stories, such as "The Tale of Peter Rabbit," are a case in point. Although they may in fact appeal to the adult reader, they are not directed at adults and contain no subtext for the adult. Other works that were originally written for adults sometimes turn out for one reason or another to become part of the corpus of children's literature. This has happened in the case of Pushkin's *skazki*, or fairy tales, which were written as adult literature and retain value as such but are now primarily considered to be part of children's literature. Swift's *Gulliver's Travels*, the original of which contains much too strong and stark stuff for children, has also become part of children's literature, in effect accidentally, by means of the many children's versions it has spawned.

A third kind of children's literature, such as Carroll's *Alice in Wonderland* and *Through the Looking Glass*, is explicitly written for *both* audiences, children and adults. The distinctive feature of such works is that they consist of a doubly encoded structure that includes one text for the adult reader and another that is designed for the child reader. This is the kind of children's literature to which Olesha's *Three Fat Men* belongs, for it is doubly encoded in exactly this way.

On closer examination, *Three Fat Men* turns out to be a multiply encoded work, because it has not only a child's text but several texts for adults. In the manner of Laurence Sterne and his latter-day popularizer, Viktor Shklovsky, Olesha further complicates the intertextuality of *Three Fat Men* by frequently commenting on his own employment of just those devices that are most characteristic of the different genres found in it. For example, through asides and apostrophes Olesha deliberately bares those narrative devices calculated to produce the greatest impression of intrigue and adventure. Perhaps most interestingly, he lays bare the fantastic nature of folktales by denying in several places that there are any miracles. Yet, he creates sequences and episodes that have a fantasticality all their own. In *Three Fat Men*, as in other works, Olesha subverts familiar conventions, devices, and motifs only so that he can use them in his own way and for his own purposes.

Shklovsky is no doubt correct in claiming for *Three Fat Men* the status of the first revolutionary tale for children. Perhaps it is revolutionary in another sense as well: that through mixing and crossing familiar generic categories and making familiar techniques strange Olesha is exploring the possible re-creation and reformulation of children's literature itself. In *Three Fat Men* Olesha has produced a metafictional, sui generis work that challenges the reader to think through its own structure, to rethink familiar generic conventions, and to see the possibility of new directions in children's literature.

A Designer's Text

When *Envy* first appeared everyone was certain that the book was something special, but to this day there is no agreement about exactly what sort of a book it is. Pertsov has asserted that *Envy* was the only work of its kind in the era it comes from,[23] yet he sheds little light on the genre to which it belongs. The very dimensions of the book, considerably less than one hundred pages long in the 1974 edition of Olesha's selected works, suggest that it is somewhere between a very long *povest'* and a very short novel. Gleb Struve believes that the novelty of *Envy* inheres in its "freshness of form and manner."[24] Struve views the work's form in the following way: "It has only six characters, of whom three stand as it were for the old world and three for the new. This bareness and simplicity of structure, reducing the theme to an almost algebraic and symbolic baldness, is obviously deliberate."[25]

Struve's analysis of *Envy*'s apparent simplicity has given way in recent Western criticism to a greater recognition of the work's inherent complexity. Reacting to the approach of Struve and others who would impute a spare directness to *Envy*'s structure, Robert Maguire has substituted a metaphor taken from the world of construction and the scaffolding Olesha describes in "The Tale of Two Brothers" (74). "Olesha erects a scaffolding that has all the stark simplicity of a formula plot: two 'old' characters (Ivan and Anechka) versus two 'new' ones (Volodia, Valia), with Kavalerov and Andrei Babichev providing the bridge. But it is a trap to catch the careless reader, and most critics, hypnotized by the symmetry, have fallen into it, reading the work as *a conventional novel of manners, not the symbolist fantasy it is*" (italics added).[26]

Maguire's reading of *Envy* as a "trap" for the reader who is willing to fall back on old, reliable, and comfortable generic expectations is particularly noteworthy, because it underlines the fact that Olesha is not simply borrowing tried and true formulae. To mix in another metaphor, Olesha is not just putting new wine, his own characters, into an old bottle, the novel of manners. On the contrary, in *Envy*, Olesha actively undermines and fights against familiar novelistic conventions. T. S. Berczynski has observed correctly that "structurally, the text displays a baroque disdain for genre lines" and that *Envy* is a novel "only in the loosest sense."[27]

Berczynski bases his argument largely on the fact that *Envy* consists of a disparate collection of materials, including "quoted verse, letters, bureaucratic memoranda, an excerpt from a pamphlet, and even a sign," as well as a story within the story, "The Tale of the Meeting of Two Brothers."[28] There are in addition various passages that are based on other extraliterary sources. A summary of the people Andrei Babichev meets one morning is done as parody of a bureaucratic list, replete with the numbers one through eight (17). The scene of the soccer match includes a section that makes use of cinematic technique. In fact, Olesha characteristically lays bare the device by explicitly comparing his description of how play stopped when the ball landed at Kavalerov's feet in the stands with a movie film breaking off and holding on a single "washed out frame" (86).[29]

The compositional techniques of *Envy* ineluctably bring to mind the devices of Shklovsky, Pil'niak, and Zamiatin. Just as these writers do, Olesha assembles parts of his text from a collection of materials that ostensibly have their origins outside of fiction. As with his predecessors, Olesha's letters and documents often have important plot-bearing functions. For example, Volodya Makarov's letter to Andrei Babichev contains not only important information about the characters and their relationships with one another but also a foreshadowing of the soccer match in which Volodya will play (45). Thus Olesha defamiliarizes, or makes strange, novelistic structure by turning it into a kind of puzzle that the reader must put together in order to make out the plot.

No Day without a Line is an important work in its own right, but it is also significant for the way in which it has made possible new readings of Olesha's previous works. There has been much talk about whether *No Day without a Line* represents a new genre. Vladimir Solov'ev is one critic who believes that it does not. He maintains that while *No Day without a Line* is itself not a new genre, its emergence has enabled us to perceive *Envy* as "a writer's notebook organized by a plot" and as an "experimental novel."[30] Certainly there are many dozens of passages in *Envy* that appear as if they would be more at home in a writer's notebook than in a novel. One of the better known of these is found in Kavalerov's musings at the end of the first chapter: "I entertain myself with observations. Have you ever paid attention to the fact that salt falls off the tip of a knife without leaving any trace . . .?" (15).

This interlude, like so many others of its ilk in *Envy*, has absolutely nothing to do with furthering the plot. In fact, it is a digression that acts to retard the plot's development. There is, of course, nothing particularly novel in novelistic digressions. What is different in Olesha is the degree to which these digressions may be perceived as extracts that have been lifted directly from the writer's notebook. It is hard to escape the distinct impression that Olesha has taken material straight from his notebook and reframed it within the structure of *Envy*'s plot. In their new structural environment the notes take on new semiotic roles. One of these, the traditional role, has primarily to do with portraying the poetic sensibility of Kavalerov in part one and of Olesha's narrative persona in part two. Yet, in *Envy*, the reader senses that what Olesha is attempting to do is to reverse the traditional expectations about the structural hierarchy that obtains in the novel.

In *Envy*, Olesha struggles against the kind of traditional novelistic structure in which descriptive passages are for the most part subordinate to the development of plot and character. Olesha's act of novelistic rebellion is to elevate his many passages of incidental observations to a status where they are not so much portraying characters and plot as competing with them for priority.

Put another way, Olesha takes what is usually conceived of as ornamental and makes it central. In this way *Envy* is a special late-blooming flower of the ornamental prosaist's novel that comes at the very end of the ornamentalist era. Like Bely, Pil'niak, and Zamiatin before him, Olesha makes the descriptions of things for their own sake a fundamental organizing principle of his work. The originality of Olesha's technique is that his descriptions have the unmistakable imprint of the writer's notebook.

As does *Three Fat Men*, Olesha's *Envy* may give a first impression of an ad hoc, eccentric structure that has come about because of the writer's relative lack of experience or inability to do things in the conventional manner. What Olesha is really doing, however, is contributing his own thesis to the ongoing dialogue made acute by such writers as Shklovsky, Pil'niak, and Zamiatin about how novels are structured. Much less obviously than *Three Fat Men*, *Envy* also contains a multiplicity of texts: the novel of manners, or its subtle parody, a symbolist fantasy, a collection of fragments and documents, and a writer's notebook. One of *Envy* 's real merits is its great potential for allowing the reader to be in effect the "designer" of the text. The point is not to determine which of these texts *Envy* really is. The point is that *Envy* is a special kind of metafiction that battles vigorously against structural and generic preconceptions that would restrict its mercurial nature.

A Limited Rejection of Belles Lettres

In 1930 Olesha wrote the following in Kornei Chukovsky's *Chukokala*, the manuscript almanac that was finally published in 1979: "Now the main point. I assert in the most decisive manner in this portentous book: *belles lettres* are doomed to perish. It is embarrassing to compose. We thirty-year-old intellectuals should write only about ourselves. We must write confessions and not novels. More important than all novels—the very highest literary work of the thirties of this century will be *Chukokala*."[31]

Despite the obvious hyperbole and the wish to please Chukovsky, the compiler of the almanac, Olesha's sentiments here with respect to belles lettres may be taken as both genuine and recurrent. Shklovsky quotes Olesha in his writer's diary as saying, "I am beginning to despise *belles lettres*, any kind of invention in literature, perhaps simply from lack of strength, from the inability to compose."[32] It certainly seems paradoxical that Olesha should profess hatred for invention, since that is manifestly one of his greatest strengths as a writer. Yet, perhaps because he stakes so much on his ability to show things from ever fresh and novel perspectives and to compose his works, if not always in outright violation of, then in constant tension with accepted conventions, it is understandable that Olesha might eventually tire of invention.

It is particularly interesting that Olesha's comments on the supposed imminent demise of belles lettres should be made in Chukovsky's *Chukokala*, because it is a book that performs on a massive scale the task Shklovsky undertakes in a work such as *Zoo, or Letters Not about Love.* That is to say, *Chukokala* is possibly the most remarkable work of metaliterature in the Soviet period. For in *Chukokala*, Chukovsky incorporates many short notes, whole poems, and observations of his contemporaries within the framework of his own text in such a way as to become their coauthor himself. Thus he carries out the same sort of assignment Shklovsky had set himself in *Zoo:* to make readers reevaluate the very processes by which literature is made. It is not surprising then that Olesha, who is himself always searching for ways and means to revitalize literary genres, should give such high praise to *Chukokala*. Implicit in Olesha's remark in *Chukokala* is the notion that the novel has become ossified as a genre and that only a work such as *Chukokala* which makes writers and readers reformulate the act of writing can bring new life to literature itself.

At the time Olesha wrote his entry in *Chukokala* he was himself engaged in a struggle to revitalize his own creative processes. In the Shklovskian manner he resorts either to nonfictional or quasi-fictional forms in order to accomplish it. In a pair of related works from 1929, "I Look into the Past" (*Ya smotriu v proshloe*) and "Human Material" (*Chelovecheskii material*), Olesha moves away from fiction in the direction of the autobiographical sketch with confessional overtones. Both of these sketches deal with Olesha's struggles with his father, who has squandered his fortune at cards and wants his son to become a successful engineer, partly to restore the family's financial position. Yet, in "Human Material" and to an extent in "I Look into the Past," Olesha's indignation at the treatment he received as a child overpowers his artistic instincts. Whereas in *Envy*, "The Cherry Stone," and other works Olesha graphically depicts the competition of contending forces between the old and young generations in terms of a dialogical struggle, in the sketches he seems content simply to indicate the outlines of that struggle rather than embody it in a convincing interaction of characters.

By the middle of the 1930s the sketch has nearly, though not entirely, taken over from the story in Olesha's work in short forms. The story "Natasha" (1936), is an exception to Olesha's strong tendency to gravitate away from fiction. Olesha's technique in many of his sketches is to build toward a culminating image that will act as a kind of climax. For instance, at the end of "Spectacles" he writes: "The younger brother of the melancholy bicycle seems evil, impatient and unsusceptible to training. It shakes with rage and snorts. If one floated like a grasshopper, transparent and fragile, then the other flies like a rocket" (276).

Olesha's partial rejection of belles lettres that is highlighted by his move to the genre of the sketch has some paradoxical and probably unintended consequences. As in "Spectacles," Olesha's technique of building the sketch toward a striking concluding image, far from eliminating invention from his work, only increases the burden on the writer of being especially inventive at certain crucial moments. As will be shown in the next chapter, there are other sketches, such as "The Stadium in Odessa," where the climactic image produces no strong effect and thereby robs the whole sketch of the impression it might have made. Furthermore, unlike works such as *Three Fat Men* and *Envy*, Olesha's sketches are for the most part utterly conventional and break no new ground. In Olesha's sketches there is generally little innovation and no sense of tension with accepted generic norms. There is, however, one dramatic and noteworthy exception to this tendency: a work called "In the World" (*V mire*) (1930), which represents an important watershed in the overall development of Olesha's creative output, particularly in his exposition of genre and form.

The Draft as Text

"In the World" is a hybrid combination of a lyrical etude, a sketch of the writer's plans for future work, and a very short story. It is comprised of several loosely arranged parts. In the beginning, the narrator is in search of the kinds of first impressions of the world around him that so many of Olesha's narrators engage in. Then comes a digression on the difficulties of writing, followed by a description of a water tower.

The following part of "In the World" contains the outlines of a story Olesha is planning to write about a beggar that, considering his talent for portraying society's outcasts, was unfortunately never fully realized. A visit to Odessa comes after the interlude about the beggar. The final section of "In the World" describes a conversation between a grandmother and her two granddaughters that the narrator overhears. There is no unifying plot to connect the different parts of "In the World." Nevertheless, the narrator's controlling voice and the theme of individual human perception of the surrounding world both act to give it a certain coherence despite the seemingly unrelated sections.

One of the major themes of "In the World" is the process of writing itself. Here Olesha tells us, "I can not think up anything in advance. Everything that I have written I wrote without a plan. Even a play. Even the adventure novel *Three Fat Men*" (234). This confession by Olesha of his inability to plan the course of his works ahead of time is a special sort of bragging, but it is meant sincerely. For Olesha's refusal to structure his works in advance was a deliberate strategy with him and a source of pride. He once told one of his contemporaries: "Don't think about the plot. It's not so important. Begin the story with how the rain began and you went with the girl into the gateway. Write about yesterday. Or you've arrived at the stadium . . . I can undertake to make a story from any beginning phrase."[33]

Olesha does not mean to suggest in "In the World" that writing is an easy task, however. On the contrary, he notes that there are three hundred drafts of the first page of *Envy*. "Possession of a writer's technique is attained by daily and systematic—like a job—writing. Alas, we don't know how to work" (237). This lament that it is hard to write is taken up by Olesha later in *No Day without a Line*, where notes of desperation and sometimes indifference are added to the difficulty the writer experiences in the pursuit of his craft.

In parts of "In the World" Olesha provides a running commentary on his own technique. An involved series of images culminates in a comparison of a tree trunk with a beam: "The beam, which is standing on its end, and which—if one stops entertaining oneself with metaphors—is simply the gray, dusty trunk of a tree" (238). Here Olesha engages in more than the technique of exposing the device. He also does more than provide an explanation or rationalization of his images, something he does frequently. He is making nothing less than a statement of his credo as a writer, because producing clever metaphors and other images was what Olesha liked to do best and what he liked best about his own work. It is even possible that his infatuation with original imagery led him to neglect other facets of his work.[34]

Always self-conscious about his own particular techniques of writing, Olesha begins in "In the World" an explicit examination of the process of writing itself. In this and many other respects, it is a harbinger and a prototype of *No Day without a Line*. It has a montage-like structure in which the different parts are often conceptually or thematically related but are not fully integrated with each other. The constituent parts themselves are similar. Both works contain introspective passages of critical self-examination, lyrical etudes and sketches, and outlines of future plans. Finally, both are in their essence writing about writing.

Viewed in the context of Olesha's poetics, "In the World" looks like nothing so much as selections that have been taken directly from the writer's notebook and published for public consumption. In this instance Olesha has combined within the framework of a single text his observations of the world around him, his constant self-commentary, and his play with technique, not by means of a loosely constructed fictional plot but rather by loosely collocated themes and motifs. Almost as though by an artistic sleight of hand Olesha has freed himself of the necessity to organize his work by traditional means of plot construction. The composition of "In the World" is reminiscent of both *Envy* and *Three Fat Men* in its extreme compositional heterogeneity. Just as in those works, Olesha manages in "In the World" to combine the apparently uncombinable. The result is not exactly a sketch and not quite a short story but a special hybrid of the two genres.

Olesha's self-conscious indulgence in his favorite devices is more than simply play for its own sake. It is symptomatic of his constant probing of the rules and boundaries of literature itself in search of recombinations and reformulations of familiar forms. The inclusion of Olesha's plans for a novel about a beggar, together with his observations on nature and the writer's craft, suggests strongly that Olesha's real innovation here is to present the reader with a draft as text.

Cineliterature and Media Crossings

During the 1920s the Russian formalists, who had already demonstrated their interest in the internal structure and dynamics of prose and poetry, began also to turn their attention to the formal properties of cinema. The formalists, such as Shklovsky, reveal a bias toward the literary genesis of film and tend to stress the connections between prose and poetry and the cinema. For example, in an article from 1927 Shklovsky perceives a distinction between movies that are largely based on prose and those that are more oriented toward poetry. There are also movies that are something of a hybrid in their combination of prose elements with poetic ones.[35] Shklovsky's literary slant may be contrasted with the work of a critic such as Kazansky, who stresses the technical and structural origins of film in photography.[36]

Olesha, whose grounding in prose is strongly felt in all of his dramatic works, has also made some extremely interesting but little known critical observations about the relationship between literature and the cinema. Writing in an introduction to the scenario *Cardinal Questions,* Olesha discusses the degree to which cinematic scenarios should be works of literature in and of themselves. Olesha believes that the stronger the literary and verbal qualities of a scenario, the better the producer can visualize it as a film and the more possibilities the director has for implementing it as such.

Echoing Shklovsky's analysis of the same work, Olesha cites the director's scenario of *The Parisienne* written by Charlie Chaplin as an example of "marvelous prose."[37] In composing his

own *A Strict Youth,* Olesha employs the same vigor and attention
to detail that he would in a short story. He even uses a metaphor
such as the "dragonfly shadow of the window panes on the walls"
in order to suggest a certain kind of light. Olesha claims that the
producer worked long and successfully to obtain just the sort of effect he had in mind. Olesha describes the process of composing a
scenario in the following way:

> In order to write with enthusiasm I have to invent the form,
> and when I write a scenario it seems to me I am writing a
> completely independent work of literature. . . . I do not forget
> for a second that what I am writing has to be turned into
> visual images.
> In this way a new genre arises. It is not drama and not
> *belles lettres.* For drama there is too much painting and for
> *belles lettres* the composition is too sparse.
> It is an original form on which the poet may work to develop
> in himself the qualities of both a dramatist and a belletrist.[38]

The miniature scenario that follows this, *Cardinal Questions,*
is written in part as an illustration of the method Olesha wishes
to practice. The scenario is about a Komsomol meeting that takes
the form of a trial of a young man who has seen and been
frightened by a ghost. It turns out that fortunately for the Komsomol members Marxist-Leninist philosophy has provided expla-
nations for things that once seemed "inexplicable and terrible."
The illusion is resolved when the young man and his girlfriend go
off to bring in the putative ghost, who had been standing in some
bushes. At the end, the young couple picks a bouquet of flowers
and kisses. This scenario is so saccharine that it leaves the reader
in a state of bewilderment over the author's complete lapse of artistic discrimination in writing it. As an attempt to evoke the
poetic side of life among young Soviet communists it is altogether
unconvincing. If one had to choose the least successful of all
Olesha's works, this one would qualify easily. As such it vitiates
Olesha's attempt to illustrate how a writer may intersperse passages of dialogue with prose in order to compose a cinematic
scenario. It is difficult to imagine who Olesha thought would perform this piece, much less who would watch it.
    As his notes on cinematic scenarios demonstrate, Olesha is
very much aware of the differences between prose and dramatic

forms. Nevertheless, he is sometimes unable to restrain himself from incorporating certain prominent features of his prose in his drama, even when it is not entirely consistent from an artistic point of view. This tendency is especially evident in connection with his portrayal of character speech in certain works. There is a tendency in Olesha's dramatic works for the author to impose his own way of seeing the world on characters of all different types. As Pertsov has noticed, even in his dramatization of *The Idiot*, the author has "Oleshanized" certain scenes that are not shown directly in the novel but are necessary for the continuity of the play.[39] In the dramatic version of *Three Fat Men* and to a lesser extent in the scenario *Walter*,[40] the speech of many of the characters, both positive and negative, is filled with the kinds of poetic images that are characteristic of the author's imagination but not necessarily of their own.

For instance, in *Three Fat Men* the General and the Cardinal, who are two of the villainous triumvirate in control of the play's imaginary kingdom, display the kind of poetic sensibility that might more appropriately be found in the heroes such as Suok and Tibul. The general reacts to the noise of the crowd of the revolutionaries who are about to take power by saying that "It's as though we were sitting inside a guitar and someone was picking the bass string" (244). The Cardinal has an equally well developed imagination, and he finds that the buzzing of the crowd is "as though we were sitting in a bomb" (246). In *Three Fat Men* perhaps Olesha is able to carry off this apparent contradiction, for in the topsy-turvy, carnivalistic logic of the play it is not out of the realm of possibility that the villains should possess a fertile imagination. The potential contradiction here is that otherwise the three fat men are shown exclusively in either a ludicrous or a deprecatory light.

Even in cases where Olesha employs imagery that is in harmony with a character's personality, a more fundamental question may arise in connection with the transfer of such imagery from its original prose environment to a new dramatic medium. In *A Conspiracy of Feelings*, for example, in Kavalerov's dream Valya tells Andrei some of the things Kavalerov has said about her: "He said that my knees were like oranges. I haven't heard such words from you."[41] Soon thereafter Valya repeats another of Olesha's favorite images to Andrei: "He said that I roared past him like a branch full of flowers and leaves" (P 69).

The original producer of *Three Fat Men*, N. M. Gorchakov, experienced considerable difficulty in trying to capture the essence of Olesha's poetic prose in scenic terms: "Scenes that sounded in reading unusually poetic, striking, and light, on the stage turned out to be empty and produced no effect at all. There where the author had a striking remark that explained the whole inner world of the characters, it turned out on stage as an unconvincing pause, a complex, clumsy change in scenery."[42]

Olesha himself came to realize the problems inherent in trying to translate the imagery and the poetry of his prose into effective dramatic form, and resolved to remedy them thus:

> An exact phrase can often get in the way on stage. This is what happened with *A Conspiracy of Feelings*, where the verbal texture of the play came apart, like plaster from a wall, covering over the play itself.
>
> Now I am considering the question: is aphoristic speech needed on stage and could not one create a full role by way of stuttering speech that jumps from one object to another. I want to create a theater of the fragile phrase.[43]

Although it was written for the screen and not the stage, *A Strict Youth* contains Olesha's resolution of the problem of character dialogue. Here the dialogue is extremely terse, and characters rarely speak more than a line or two to each other, and often no more than a word or two. Such is the case in scene 22, where the young people are at a training session at the stadium and they are talking about the hero, Grisha Fokin:

> FIRST YOUNG MAN. He compiled the third "GTO" complex.
> SECOND YOUNG MAN. Who compiled it?
> THIRD. What kind of complex?
> FIRST YOUNG MAN. A moral one.
> THIRD. What does it mean?
> GIRL. Don't you understand?
> THIRD. No. (310)

In some of his dramatic works, particularly in *A Strict Youth* and *Walter*, Olesha, attempts to create the image of tough, nononsense characters who know what they want and what they want to say. Olesha's terse style of dialogue suits the portrayal of such characters well. At times, however, the dynamism inherent in Olesha's short bursts of character speech is impaired by a certain woodenness of expression and a tendency toward the use of clichés. For example, in the dialogue just quoted from *A Strict Youth* the characters discuss the spiritual qualities that the GTO complex is supposed to develop. It turns out that the elimination of the power of money has made possible the transformation of qualities formerly considered bourgeois, such as sentimentality and sincerity, so that they now receive their true expression. This theme, which was one of Olesha's favorites during the middle of the 1930s, reflects his constant desire simultaneously to justify the best of past traditions and to discover the best in contemporary socialist values.

> FIRST YOUNG MAN. The bourgeoisie corrupted these concepts. Because there was the power of money.
> GIRL (quickly). And now that there isn't the power of money, all these feelings receive their full purity. Don't you understand? (311)

The problem here is that Olesha's dialogue loses some of its sparkle as it moves off in the direction of the platitudes of socialist realism. Even some of the first readers of selections from *A Strict Youth* that were published in the newspaper *Literaturnaia gazeta* on 24 June 1934 felt that Olesha's characters moralized too much and acted too little. Olesha defends himself on the grounds that he wants to depict the nobility of Soviet youth. "I consider that we should generalize, see the best, idealize. I want to see only the good."[44]

Olesha also has recourse to his perception of the difference between prose and cinema as a means of putting his work in the best light: "I want you to remember that this is not a novel and not a novella, it is a scenario for a film. . . . in this picture much will receive a more full-blooded life. That which is conceived as irony will be ironic, much that seems categorical in reading will acquire a comic nuance on the screen and so on. The film will be more concrete than what is written as prose."[45]

Parts of *A Strict Youth* actually appear to be only a skeleton on which the producer will need to fill out the flesh. The laconicism of the characters' speech is matched by the style of the passages in *A Strict Youth* that are devoted to cinematic directions. Olesha's penchant for pithy brevity finds its ultimate expression in the passages of *A Strict Youth* that are from a literary point of view narrative and from a cinematic point of view directions. The scenario begins thus:

A garden.
A veranda.
A table on the veranda.
Four settings.
Festive service.
A hot day. Movement of leaves and shadows.
Dragonfly shadow of the window panes on the wall.
The house is surrounded by a garden. (299)

One-word lines and sentences abound in *A Strict Youth.* For example, in the Russian text the twenty-first scene contains ten lines, seven of which consist of a single word:

Morning.
At the stadium.
Walkways, Crosswalks
Stairs.
Tracks.
Playing areas.
Grass.
Trees.
Signs.
Numbers written in lime in the sand. (310)

For the most part, Olesha succeeds in *A Strict Youth*, where he fails in *Cardinal Questions.* In the former scenario the interposition of cinematic directions with dialogue is carried out with precision and purpose, so that when it is read as a work of literature it is artistically coherent within itself. Pertsov believes that the original director, A. Room, did not exhaust the profundity of Olesha's scenario and that it still awaits its producer.[46] It appears, however, that any future producer will have to be fairly liberal in blunting the excessively moralistic tone of the screenplay for it to have any chance of making an impact on audiences as a film.

In addition to transferring his poetic imagery from its original prose medium to drama, Olesha also attempted at least one other noteworthy innovation in his implementation of dramatic structure: to dispense with acts and substitute for them an interconnected sequence of scenes. Meyerhold, who staged the first production of *A List of Blessings* and even made some important contributions to the play itself,[47] reacted with some skepticism to Olesha's dramatic techniques: "Olesha's dramaturgical conception is not entirely usual. His approach is complicated by not so typical scenic skills, which perhaps he doesn't have. For him the scenic situation is not so important—for him all the thoughts which he wants to convey through this construction are what is important."[48]

Olesha's dramatic works contain many of the same poetic impulses that his prose does. In drama, as elsewhere, Olesha wages an ongoing battle against conventional structure and form. He also does not hesitate to adapt techniques and elements of one medium in another. Yet, his attempt to infuse dramatic dialogue with his highly poetic and lyrical imagery that is so effective in its prose context tends to fall flat in dramatic exposition. Also, the effort at reforming dramatic structure yields little of significance.

Although Gleb Struve detects some similarities with Ibsen, as well as some of the attributes of symbolist drama in *A List of Blessings*,[49] there is little in Olesha that puts one in mind of the major movements such as symbolist, expressionist, or absurdist drama. The one area where Olesha is clearly in contact with contemporary dramatic practice is that of slapstick comedy. In *Three Fat Men* Olesha develops slapstick humor to genuinely hilarious proportions. One can only lament that he did not pursue his exploitation of slapstick more fully elsewhere.

No Day without a Line and Metaliterature

Can we say to what genre *No Day without a Line* belongs? First, it should be noted that since the book consists of posthumously published selections from Olesha's notebooks, the problem of what comprises the canonical text is to some degree unresolved. Few of those closest to Olesha seem convinced that the book's present form is necessarily its final one. Gladkov definitely does not consider *No Day without a Line* as it is presently constituted to be canonical, because it could continue to grow if more material from Olesha's archives were included.[50] Shklovsky is also emphatic in his opinion on this matter: "It is not completely assembled. At least a quarter of the book has not been published. We were not able to make out the structure of the book completely."[51]

A comparison of the 1965 and 1974 editions of *No Day without a Line* indicates that the latter contains a number of passages that are fuller than the earlier one. On the other hand, there is at least one passage from the 1965 edition that was deleted in 1974.[52] A curious anomaly concerns a large portion of Olesha's notes that his wife, Olga Suok-Olesha, published in the newspaper *Literaturnaia gazeta* on 19 September 1973. In an accompanying note Suok-Olesha writes that the notes appearing in the newspaper are to be part of the expanded edition of *No Day without a Line.* But only part of the selection excerpted by Suok-Olesha in *Literaturnaia gazeta* was actually published in the 1974 edition. What is left out is an entry dated from 1940 in which Olesha describes a soccer match between "Spartak" and "TsDKA" (an abbreviation for "Central Home of the Red Army"), which was also attended by Andrei Starostin and Fadeev. Olesha is, as usual, captivated by the match itself, but he is dismayed by the crowds that attend the big matches: "Ladies, famous people eat sandwiches, arrive late, stand in the walkways, and call out to friends." This entry is important because it demonstrates that Olesha continued to take an active interest in soccer long after his youth. It also contains a much less romantic depiction of soccer than the one found in his notes about the early days of Odessan soccer. This omission is particularly surprising in light of the fundamental role of sport in Olesha's life, literature, and view of the world.

As it is presently constructed, *No Day without a Line* consists of five chapters, "Childhood" (*Detstvo*), "Moscow," "Odessa," "The Golden Shelf" (*Zolotaia polka*), and "The Astonishing Intersection" (*Udivitel'nyi perekrestok*). Because Olesha's tendency to compose his works using the principle of montage reaches its fullest expression in *No Day without a Line,* it seems unlikely that any two readers or critics would ever agree on the book's optimum structure. For instance, certain passages in the earlier chapters that deal with literature might well have been included in "The Golden Shelf," which is primarily devoted to a discussion of Olesha's favorite authors and works. On the other hand, these passages are by no means out of place where they stand, and in fact they are an important part of Olesha's youth. For the most part, the present form of *No Day without a Line* gives both chronological sequence and thematic coherence to the large body of Olesha's notes, which in the published form of *No Day without a Line* comprise by far his longest single work.

The subject matter of *No Day without a Line* is extremely diverse. It contains extensive observations on literature, including both his own work and the work of others. There are several independent sketches. Discussions of future plans are common. Memoiristic passages occupy an especially large and important place. The autobiographical passages describe a whole spectrum of cultural phenomena and institutions, including the circus, soccer, the reception of new technology and the cinema, descriptions of celebrities such as Max Linder and the parachutist Ernest Vitollo, and the beginnings of organized physical education, when tennis balls and rackets were the most valuable equipment.

Olesha himself was acutely aware of the somewhat indeterminate nature of his work's structure. He vacillated between concern that his notes were not leading to anything and confidence that they would eventually culminate in something finished. On one hand he writes, "In the future I will have to try to conduct these notes so that something completed will result. If there is no completion, what do they represent?" (453). In another place, however, he asserts: "The reader should not think that this book, however visually it consists of separate pieces on different themes, is, so to speak, only extended in length; no, it is rounded; if you wish, it is a book that even has a plot, and a very interesting one. There lived a man and he lived to old age. There is the plot. An interesting plot, even a fantastic one. Indeed, to live to old age is a fantastic thing" (458).

Here Olesha invites the reader to read *No Day without a Line* as a text about the life of the author. Usually, such a story would be considered among the most ordinary and conventional possible texts. Yet, Olesha wants the reader to perceive this apparently mundane story in a fantastic light. (To survive to old age the time of Stalin was for some indeed fantastic.) This passage might be taken as representative of Olesha's poetics on the whole, because it exhorts the reader to reinterpret the everyday as something quite exceptional. It is also indicative of the conscious manner in which Olesha carries on his struggle against established generic models in *No Day without a Line.* This attitude is also evident in a passage where Olesha claims that he could write novels in the manner of Tolstoy and Goncharov but that to do so would be a waste of time (426). Olesha has in mind a new structure for the modern model: "Contemporary prose pieces can have value that corresponds to the contemporary mentality only when they are written at one sitting. A thought or a reminiscence of twenty or thirty lines, let's say one hundred lines maximum, that is the contemporary novel" (342).

Olesha's definition of the modern novel should not be taken literally but rather as a provocative way of justifying his own poetics. Here he is in effect acknowledging that what his friend Mikhail Zoshchenko had said about his work was true: that Olesha's best form is "little remarks, scraps, little pieces, or something like a short story (novella), but not a short story."[53] Olesha is also making explicit what was only implicit in an earlier work such as *Envy*, namely, that the canons of nineteenth-century realism are no longer productive in the modern era. They need to be revitalized and reformulated. As we can see from his observations and the many independent sketches in *No Day without a Line*, Olesha will focus his efforts on the microstructures of his work. The macrostructure will be left largely to take care of itself, that is, for the reader to fashion for him- or herself, with only occasional suggestions from Olesha about how a plot might be deduced from these microstructures.

It should come as no surprise that Viktor Shklovsky was keenly interested in the structural properties of *No Day without a Line*. After all, as noted here, Shklovsky actually helped to give the book its final form. This act would seem to give Shklovsky's career a fitting symmetry, for in putting together *No Day without a Line*, Shklovsky and his colleagues Belinkov and Gromov were really taking the techniques of framing and reframing he had used decades before in *Zoo* or *Letters Not about Love* to their logical conclusion. In this way they become the ultimate (collective) author as framer, since all and not just some of the material in *No Day without a Line* is someone else's. Thus, the question of who exactly is the author, that is, who is responsible for the way in which the plot is finally constructed, is even further complicated by the special history of the book's publication. Yet, in writing about *No Day without a Line* Shklovsky treats Olesha as the sole author.

Shklovsky marvels at the success of *No Day without a Line* in constructing the "plot on the internal juxtapositions of moments apparently grasped capriciously."[54] He is not content merely with describing the internal workings of Olesha's book, and he finds in them a higher meaning and purpose: "Art always goes away from itself, destroys the past in order to return to it with a new understanding. The construction of new systems of plot that replace the old ones is a great and ancient task."[55] Knowing what we know about Shklovsky's role in *No Day without a Line*, it is impossible not to note that Shklovsky's remarks contain a certain implicit reflexivity. At the least, what he says about Olesha's book is exactly what he would like to have said about his own work.

Shklovsky's implication that *No Day without a Line* represents the formation of a new system of plot needs to be examined further. The fragmentary structure of *No Day without a Line* has antecedents in Russian literature. As has been pointed out, Vasily Rozanov's works are important models for the technique of composition by fragments. There are other links between Olesha and Rozanov. The candid, confessional qualities of *No Day without a Line* bring to mind the notorious and often embarrassing frankness of Rozanov. And in *No Day without a Line*, just as in Rozanov's works, the presence of the author-narrator may be strongly felt throughout. Yury Ivask's observation about Rozanov in *A Secluded Place* and *Fallen Leaves*, that "His own 'I' is the main hero,"[56] could be applied just as aptly to Olesha in *No Day without a Line*. It should be pointed out, however, that except for Olesha's remarks on literature his subject matter is largely unlike that of Rozanov. Also, the aphoristic quality of Rozanov's work finds little or no response in Olesha and is more of a model for Andrei Sinyavsky-Tertz's *Thoughts Unaware* (*Mysli vrasplokh*) (1966), also a candid work that is a series of fragments.

Even though Olesha eagerly battles against the standards of nineteenth-century realism, he is himself aware that his work is not novel in any absolute sense. He cites as one of his inspirations Marcel Proust's *Remembrance of Things Past*: "I would like to pass through life backwards as Marcel Proust succeeded in doing in his time" (377). Elizabeth Beaujour has pointed out that Proust does not really "go backwards through life, he brings past time forward to the present." Furthermore, whereas "for Olesha the original sensation is primary, for Proust the value lies in the remembered sensation."[57] According to Beaujour, *No Day without a Line* is closer to the genre of the *journal intime*. Such a work focuses neither on times of joy nor on times of great difficulty but rather on "those moments when a writer feels that there is a spring broken within him."[58] In addition, the narrative persona of a *journal intime* always carries with him a premonition of death and often feels himself to be in a state of disintegration. Olesha does in fact note his supposed "inability to write" (365) during the course of *No Day without a Line.* Beaujour also finds Olesha's depiction of himself as a broken-down athlete (457) to be particularly emblematic of his "mutilated and fragmented talent."[59]

Beaujour has shown persuasively that *No Day without a Line* does indeed have important affinities with the *journal intime.* Nevertheless, perhaps she stresses too much the motifs of failure and disintegration in *No Day without a Line.* For Olesha also describes certain moments of triumph. And even in those places where Olesha's narrative persona apparently bemoans the diminution of his talent for writing, he is often doing so with the real purpose of highlighting the regeneration of his skills for creating stimulating imagery: "I am ill. I have an illness of the sentence: suddenly in the third or fourth link it sags. . . . I see this belly sticking out below almost concretely" (344). Olesha also fairly revels in his successes: "When they rehearse this play, I see how well in general *A List of Blessings* was written. Here one might even go further and apply the words: what a remarkable work it was!" (450). Similarly, Olesha asserts that in *Envy* he has written a book "that will live for the ages" (451).

Olesha frequently pictures himself not as a wreck or a failure but as someone who occupies a special place in the universe. This feeling is expressed with great clarity in the last words of *No Day without a Line:* "I was always on the tip of a sunbeam" (558). The essence of Olesha is neither triumph nor despair but rather his vacillation between the two poles. As will be shown here subsequently in some detail, the several thematic antitheses of *No Day without a Line,* such as disintegration versus regeneration, compete with each other in a dialogical struggle that is never ultimately won by either side.

In examining the structure of *No Day without a Line* it is important to keep in mind that this book contains not a single text but a multiplicity of different texts. In this connection it is particularly illuminating to consider Gary Saul Morson's analysis of Dostoevsky's *Diary of a Writer* (*Dnevnik pisatelia*) as a work of metaliterature:

Dostoevsky's *Diary* . . . juxtaposes traditional literary and non-literary material, combines apparently incompatible genres, and frustrates the search for the pattern it intimates in order to examine the nature of literary unity and structure. . . . The *Diary* "impedes," "defamiliarizes," and so renders "perceptible" the ways in which readers usually identify structure and infer meaning. . . . The *Diary* is not lawless, but systematically unlawful, a sort of negative exemplification of the conventions it ostentatiously defies.[60]

Morson adds that the pattern of Dostoevsky's *Diary* is "unfulfilled plans, apologies, self-justifications, and revised plans."[61] Morson's description of *Diary* directly characterizes Olesha's *No Day without a Line* to a remarkable degree. Not only does *No Day without a Line* combine usually incompatible genres such as sketches, literary critiques, and reminiscences; it also is filled with all sorts of plans that were never realized, statements of belief and intent, and a whole range of self-justifying remarks of the kind just discussed. Perhaps most important, Olesha's long-time defiance of traditional literary conventions and his tendency to be "systematically unlawful" reaches its apogee in *No Day without a Line.*

The essence of metaliterature is its reflexivity and the self-conscious way in which it regards itself.[62] Olesha's numerous self-conscious comments on the plan, or lack of one, for *No Day without a Line* epitomize the way in which the whole book ubiquitously probes the nature and the limits of literary structure. At the same time Olesha constantly "defamiliarizes" and "impedes" the ways in which the reader perceives the book's structure and meaning. Perhaps the most overt example of this technique concerns a comparison Olesha makes between two things he has seen, a sparrow walking alone on a slope and a mortally wounded thief. Olesha follows this comparison by exposing its mechanism with a disclaimer: "I do not want the reader to seek in my book any sort of analogies that have been thought up ahead of time, any conceptual correspondences. If they come about on their own, that's all right, that's their business. Consciously I am most of all far from a wish somehow baldly to philosophize beginning with a sparrow and jumping across to a thief" (459).

Olesha reveals here the method behind his technique of composition by montage. The effect of this disclaimer is, of course, to make the reader want to discover just what really is the connection between the two events. In order to do this one has to turn to an earlier entry in *No Day without a Line* in which Olesha describes an incident he witnessed, when a thief lay on the ground after being shot in a failed attempt at robbery: "His only life, the life given to him once for millions, for hundreds of millions, for millions of millions of years, was coming to an end. I remember that rising mountain of his chest, that whole world, that whole independent, gigantic universe, greater perhaps than our own, greater than all of the millions, greater perhaps because it is separate and independent" (427).

In light of this passage the relationship between the dying thief and the sparrow takes on a discernible form. The sparrow, like the thief, is alone in the world. He is completely absorbed in his own activity and goes about his business without paying any attention to the people and things around him. It is this very independence and individuality that gives him, just as it gives the thief, his special worth in Olesha's eyes.

Olesha's technique of naked juxtaposition in his miniature sketch about the sparrow and the thief forces the reader to decipher the author's meaning from bits of evidence scattered about the text. In this way Olesha dramatically maximizes the estrangement and difficulty inherent in the reading of his work. Nowhere else does Olesha give the reader so much freedom—and so much responsibility—to design the meaning and the structure of the text for him- or herself.

No Day without a Line represents a logical culmination in the development of Olesha's poetics. Within its framework the miniature observation of the writer's notebook, always a central feature in Olesha, now assumes a position of utmost, even governing priority. Plot, which Olesha had the ability to create, as *Three Fat Men* clearly shows, but which he was little interested in, has virtually been done away with altogether. By announcing what the plot is, but not actually constructing one, Olesha gives over most of his plot-making rights to the reader. It seems most appropriate, then, that *No Day without a Line* should have been ended, that is, assembled by others. It is also fitting that the book's final form remains in a real sense open-ended since, as discussed earlier, it is still subject to further additions from Olesha's notes.

The ongoing struggles with and discussions of the rules of fictional genres of the early Olesha have broadened in *No Day without a Line* to include a battle with the conventions of literature in general. At the same time, these struggles, which are largely covert in a work such as *Envy*, have become overt in *No Day without a Line*. Olesha, who always felt constrained by the traditional conventions of the novel, makes a complete break with them in *No Day without a Line*. For Olesha a microsketch, a confession, or a diary with a plot may take the place of the novel altogether.

Olesha's apparently fast and loose play with the definition of the novel should not be viewed as a writer's impressionistic understanding of something scholars of literature might define more precisely. It is rather part of his effort to liberate himself from rules others have made and to give his work its own order, its own rationale. In *No Day without a Line*, Olesha has not only finally found his most natural, most congenial form, but he has produced his most ambitious metaliterary creation.

2 /
Variations on the Carnival

Bakhtin on the Carnival

The major proponent of the notion of carnivalistic literature is the Soviet critic Mikhail Bakhtin.[1] According to Bakhtin, beginning in classical antiquity and continuing over the course of thousands of years, the spirit of the carnival and many of its features and images became transposed into certain literary genres, particularly Menippean satire, creating in effect a "carnivalized" or carnivalistic literature. Eventually the carnival itself came to lose its direct influence on literature, and from about the end of the seventeenth century carnivalistic literature became the principal bearer of the carnival tradition. In this regard Bakhtin considers Rabelais and Cervantes to be particularly important. Subsequently the traits of carnivalistic literature may be found primarily in fiction that is related to the tradition of Menippean satire.[2]

While the carnival displays considerable variety over the course of time and in different places, and scholars place different degrees of emphasis on certain features of the carnival, Bakhtin's analysis is particularly relevant here since he is concerned specifically with the relationship between literature and the carnival. In Bakhtin's view the four major features of the carnival are "free familiar contact between people"; eccentricity, which gives life in the carnival the quality of being "out of the rut" and "inside out"; carnival mésalliances, such as the combination of high and low, wise and foolish; and various kinds of profanation, including indecencies and blasphemies of respected authorities.[3]

Another powerful element of the carnival is laughter, which, like eccentricity, makes possible things that cannot be done in serious times. Laughter in the carnival is ambivalent and may take the form either of ridiculing laughter or rejoicing laughter. Laughter may also act in the service of parody, which takes many forms, such as the various parodic doubles of the carnival.[4] Parody in the carnival is extremely diverse, and as

Bakhtin notes, acted as a "whole system of curved mirrors—which enlarged, miniaturized, and distorted in various directions and in various degrees."[5]

The central act of the carnival is the mock crowning and discrowning of the carnival king, who is often a fool or jester of some sort.[6] The main impulse of the carnival for change and renewal finds its expression exactly in this crowning and discrowning of the carnival king. Just as crowning and discrowning are ambivalent and dualistic in that they combine opposites within themselves, so do other images of the carnival contrast opposites, such as age and youth and front and back. In the carnival numerous paired images are formed both on the principle of similarity and the basis of contrast.[7]

In works of carnivalistic literature the major characteristics of the carnival are naturally likely to be recast, recombined, and reinterpreted in various ways. Bakhtin notes that the central dualistic carnival image of crowning and discrowning has had a great influence on literature.[8] This image is often expressed in a kind of unmasking of a character. For Bakhtin, the quintessential author of carnivalistic literature in the nineteenth century is Dostoevsky. Among other things, Dostoevsky's use of an intimate authorial stance vis-à-vis his characters, his frequent employment of parodic doubles, such as the satellites surrounding Raskolnikov, Stavrogin, and Ivan Karamazov, and his frequent exploitation of scandal scenes, which are filled with the imagery of the carnival square, are all directly or indirectly related to the tradition of the carnival and carnivalistic literature.[9]

Olesha's works do not uniformly display the many attributes of the carnival. In certain works, such as *Three Fat Men* and *Envy*, the carnival plays a central, even governing role, so that a description of their poetics is necessarily incomplete without reference to the carnival. In Olesha's stories and dramatic works, on the other hand, often only certain aspects of a carnivalistic attitude toward life are found. Nevertheless, with the possible exception of *No Day without a Line*, significant manifestations of the carnival permeate Olesha's work in all of its several different forms and genres. Since it is possible to say that with Olesha most roads lead (often backwards) to *Envy*, and *Envy* is clearly his most thoroughly carnivalistic work, the analysis here will move from those works in which the carnival is less fully developed to the novel.

The Circus as Carnival

The kernel of *Three Fat Men* is contained in a play called *Play at Execution (Igra v plakhu)* that Olesha had published already in 1922.[10] *Play at Execution* is in many respects a miniature foretaste of *Three Fat Men*. It is a one-act play that takes place on the day after the leader of a revolutionary movement has been executed by the king of an imaginary kingdom located in a port. (This port is no doubt inspired by Odessa.) Three professional actors, Ganimeed, Bartholomew, and Andrew put on a play within the play in which they convince the king to act out a scene with them in which he is executed. The climax takes place when Ganimeed, having got the king to submit his head for a mock execution, actually chops it off. Olesha's use of verse here, which displays an *a-b-a-b* rhyme scheme, produces a sing-song quality that is strongly incongruous with the action that takes place.[11] He is also little concerned with verisimilitude, as the sequence of events in *Play at Execution* is most improbable. The real impetus behind this short play and also behind *Three Fat Men* is the desire to capture the essence of revolution in terms of literary archetypes, using imaginary, fairy tale–like kingdoms and stylized kings or rulers.

At the heart of both *Play at Execution* and *Three Fat Men* is a carnival reversal in which a king or kings are made to play the role of fools. In *Play at Execution* the king goes along with all of the suggestions of the actors and even deludes himself into believing that he too is an actor. The single king of *Play at Execution* is clearly a precursor to the three fat rulers of the later novel. There is also a crowd in *Play at Execution* that foreshadows the crowd in *Three Fat Men*. In both the crowds are the revolutionary masses that are waiting in the wings to take power from their despotic rulers. And in both there is of course a happy ending in which the people reign triumphant. In *Three Fat Men* Olesha has substituted circus performers for the actors of *Play at Execution* and greatly increased the cast of characters and the scope of the action.

As already noted, since *Three Fat Men* is extremely eclectic in its borrowing from different genres and sources, it might well be asked what if anything gives the novel structural coherence. First of all, despite the fact that he claims in "In the World" not to have planned anything ahead of time (234), and despite the use of several flashbacks in time, Olesha employs an action-filled plot that leads resolutely to a climax in which the three fat men are overthrown by the revolutionary forces lead by Prospero and Tibul. At the same time, the varied constituent parts of the novel that derive from the cinema, folktales, and modern children's literature interact harmoniously and effectively because they mesh well with the novel's prevailing carnivalistic tenor.

Virtually all of Olesha's important works take place either in summer or spring, and *Three Fat Men* is no exception. At its beginning Doctor Gaspar Arneri goes out for a walk: "This time the day was marvelous: the sun did nothing but shine; the grass was so green that a feeling of sweetness even appeared in your mouth; dandelions flew about, birds whistled; and a light breeze fluttered like an airy ball gown" (98).

For Olesha the natural setting is an indispensable means of creating a holiday or carnival atmosphere. Almost invariably such a setting includes the motif of green grass. This green grass may symbolize youth, as it does in *Envy*, or the regeneration of nature, as it does in Olesha's description of spring in Odessa in *No Day without a Line*, where he writes, "The field was already turning green in those days of spring!" (416). In his speech at the First Congress of the Soviet Writers Union, Olesha associates green grass with the regeneration of his own youth. When he comes upon a hole in a wall and sees the greenery through it, he feels that "I have become young" (P 327). Green grass, with its various related connotations of youth, spring, and regeneration, becomes a central feature of Olesha's outlook on the world and a symbol both of his inner, personal spring carnivals and his outer, literary spring carnivals.

In *Three Fat Men* the motif of green grass and summery weather takes on explicitly carnivalistic overtones when it is linked with the setting for much of the novel's action, Star Square. Both in the carnival and in carnivalized literature the public square, or one of its analogues, is the locus for many of the important events.[12]

In *Three Fat Men*, Star Square has a further indirect link with the carnival, for the square is described as a "colossal circus." The circus, together with such holidays such as Mardi Gras, is one of the last remnants in modern society of the medieval carnival. However attenuated, however corrupted, the circus retains some of the imagery and the motifs of the traditional carnival: its colorful dress, its mockery of authority in the form of the clowns' comic dialogues, and its pervasive eccentricity, particularly in the behavior of the clowns, who constantly flout the rules of conventional behavior. Just this life out of the ordinary rut together with the flouting of the laws of physics engaged in by circus performers, such as the acrobats and tightrope walkers, enthralled Olesha. He returns to the theme of the circus a number of times in the sketches "At the Circus" (*V tsirke*) (1929) and "Spectacles" (*Zrelishcha*) (1937), as well as in *No Day without a Line*.

Motifs from the circus are ubiquitous throughout *Three Fat Men* and are one of the primary contributors to the novel's predominant carnival spirit. Two of the major characters, Suok and Tibul, the tightrope walker, are circus performers. Early in the novel Tibul escapes from the soldiers of the three fat men by performing a spectacular feat of tightrope walking in Star Square.

The crowd that gathers in Star Square to witness the beginnings of the revolution against the tyranny of the three fat men and Tibul's escape by tightrope displays the kinds of mésalliances typical of the carnival. It includes tradesmen, sailors, wealthy citizens, merchants, "emaciated foul-tongued actors," and little children. In *Three Fat Men* the characters are for the most part members of one or two distinct groups. In one camp there are the fat people, who are aligned with the three fat men and who tend to be wealthy and frivolous. In the other camp are the thin people, who are hard-working and honest.

In this pairing of thin and fat people Olesha crystallizes one of the major motifs of the carnival that arises out of the juxtaposition of Carnival with Lent. The bloated fat man, who is festooned with sausages and other food, represents Carnival. He is contrasted with a thin old woman, who is dressed in black and covered with fish and who stands for Lent. In England her place was taken by a male "Jack o' Lent."[13] The order of ascendancy between the thin and the fat in *Three Fat Men* corresponds with that of the carnival. As in the spring carnival, where Carnival is about to yield to Lent, the fat men of Olesha's novel are about to give way to their thin successors.

The three fat men themselves are distinguished by stupidity, cruelty, and, above all, gluttony. Their whole lives are arranged in such a way that they can overeat to the greatest possible extent. Their behavior in this respect amounts to an hyperbolic expression of the pervasive carnival motif of gluttony. In much the same manner, the three fat men are parodic depictions of the traditional impostor carnival king who is ritually discrowned. When the revolutionary forces take over, they put the three fat men in a cage previously used to hold captive the opponents of the regime. By placing the three fat men in this cage, Prospero and Tibul subject them to the ridicule of the public. Ridicule, albeit in a form lacking the full carnivalistic ambivalence characteristic of *Envy*, is indeed one of the chief governing principles of the novel. Olesha demonstrates the absurdity of the three fat men and their followers by constantly holding them up to ridicule and placing them in ridiculous situations.

The public celebration that takes place after the victory over the three fat men is described as "an unprecedented holiday" (*nebyvalyi prazdnik*) (186). These are the exact words with which Olesha describes the soccer match in *Envy*, and they form a good example of the way in which Olesha employs identical motifs in different works.

Another motif found both in *Envy* and in *Three Fat Men* concerns the gluttony that is portrayed in both novels. As in *Envy*, where Andrei is a sausage maker, there is a reference to sausage makers in *Three Fat Men*. This is not to say, however, that the same motifs in the two different novels perform the same functions or have the same connotations. In general Olesha's exploitation of carnivalistic motifs and a carnivalesque ambience in *Three Fat Men* is more overt than in *Envy* but considerably less profound. The discrowning of the false carnival kings, the three fat men, the ridiculing laughter of the crowds, even the motif of gluttony, lack the ambivalence inherent in the exposition of these motifs in *Envy*. In addition, the complex character relationships of *Envy*, which are also filled with carnivalistic ambivalence, have no parallel in *Three Fat Men*, where the characters are consistently portrayed in black and white terms. While *Three Fat Men* displays a thoroughly carnivalistic ambience of gaiety, festivity, and eccentricity, it has none of *Envy*'s carnivalistic duality and ambiguity.

Three Fat Men is a vastly different sort of novel from *Envy*. Even though the carnivalistic spirit of *Three Fat Men* does not display the complexity or the range it possesses in *Envy*, it is as essential to the former work as it is to the latter. For the carnival spirit of *Three Fat Men* is just that indispensable ingredient that gives the novel's disparate elements unity. The light-hearted side of the carnival spirit manifest in *Three Fat Men* contains within itself most of the major features intrinsic to such diverse things as slapstick comedy, folktales, and modern children's stories. It embraces the absurdity and humor of cinematic comedy, the fantasy of folktales, and the nonsense of children's literature. Thus does the carnival spirit of *Three Fat Men* bind the novel's different elements together into a poetically coherent whole.

Private Holidays and Public Spectacles

Olesha is one of the real masters of the short story in the Soviet period, despite the fact that his reputation as a short story writer is based on only a handful of stories. In a letter to Olesha, his friend and contemporary Mikhail Zoshchenko, the great Soviet satirist, expresses his appreciation for the power of Olesha's short works: "Every two of your lines are better than a whole pile of books. That's the sort of feeling I have when I read you."[14] Zoschehenko's evaluation is particularly apt, because it highlights the fact that in Olesha's best stories every line, every phrase, every image is crafted and polished to a remarkable degree. In stories such as "Liompa" (1928), "The Chain" (*Tsep'*) (1928), "Love" (*Liubov'*) (1928), and "The Cherry Stone" (*Vishnevaia kostocha*) (1929), Olesha achieves a level of artistic power and richness that places them in the company of the work of the greatest twentieth-century Russian short story writers, such as Babel and Zamiatin.

Andrew Barratt has suggested that Olesha's stories are weaker than *Envy* because in the stories the important issues raised in the novel are either trivialized or evaded.[15] Certainly Olesha's later stories suffer greatly by comparison with *Envy*. The early stories, however, have a rationale of their own that brooks favorable comparison with anything Olesha has written. For if the stories are less oriented toward the kinds of issues described in *Envy*, it is partly because the genre of the short story is less well suited to the delineating of broad social and ideological questions than the novel and partly because the stories focus primarily on questions of an intensely personal nature. Nevertheless, there are many things in common between *Envy* and the short stories. In both Olesha treats the relationship between the older and younger generations from various angles, and in both the competition between artistic sensitivity and the developing Soviet society figures prominently. Numerous motifs, such as strolls in grassy green parks, infantile points of view, and the characters' thinking in images, may be found in both *Envy* and the stories.

Perhaps the principal difference between *Envy* and the stories is one of scale. Because the stories deal primarily with highly personal situations and problems, there is a tendency in them for the scope of broader social implications to be reduced. An important exception to this trend is the story "The Cherry Stone," which treats the relationship between the individual and society in quite a direct fashion.

The setting of the stories is also typically greatly reduced by comparison with that of Olesha's short novels. Whereas the most important dramatic moments of *Envy* and *Three Fat Men* are acted out in the public square, in the early stories major events, or often only perceptions of events, take place in small, out-of-the-way places. In *Envy*, Kavalerov confronts Andrei Babichev at the airfield and in the street, but in "Love" Shuvalov and the color-blind man conduct their dialogue in a park, far from any crowds of people.

The smaller scale of the setting in many of the stories discourages or even precludes the involvement of large groups of people as witnesses to the struggles between characters. Consequently, the carnivalistic ambience that is so prominent in *Envy* and *Three Fat Men* is greatly muted in the stories, but it is not entirely lost. The carnivalistic sensibility of the stories, in keeping with their overall tenor, is manifested primarily on a highly personal level. In the stories the characters construct private, miniature carnivalistic worlds for themselves where the usual rules of behavior and perception are suspended and replaced by rules largely of their own making. In the story "Love," for example, Shuvalov tells Lelya that "I'm beginning to think in images. Laws cease to exist for me" (198). In the world Shuvalov creates for himself everything is touching and funny, and gravity no longer exists. His thoughts begin to materialize, and a wasp that enters the room becomes the tiger his imagination sees it as. The fact that Shuvalov is apparently living in a world apart from others is highlighted by his and Lelya's ability to know each other's thoughts.

Shuvalov's experience of life out of the usual rut with rules all its own is largely one of his own invention under the influence of his infatuation with Lelya. His state contrasts with that of the color-blind man whom he meets and for whom a different set of laws is not a matter of choice but rather an unavoidable condition. As is so often the case with Olesha, Shuvalov's ability to think in images is a mixed blessing, for as well as its potential to create a world of new and different dimensions for its possessor, it also imposes the burden of seeing things with an unbearable acuteness. Overwhelmed by the force love exerts on his imagination, Shuvalov proposes to the color-blind man that they exchange positions and burdens: "Give me your iris and take my love" (202).[16] When the color-blind man sneaks up on Shuvalov and Lelya in the bushes and offers to make the exchange, Shuvalov dismisses him with the words "Go eat your blue pears." Shuvalov's rejoinder here is an affirmation that he is able to distinguish between the ordinary world of the everyday and the extraordinary world of his imagination. Furthermore, he is able to choose for himself when he will take part in which one. By comparison with *Envy*, "Love" appears to be a rather optimistic story. In *Envy* the adventures of Kavalerov and Ivan in a world of fancy and imagination end up in a grubby ménage à trois with the blubbery Anechka. In "Love," Shuvalov has both an entry into a world with different rules and an easy exit back to the everyday.

The consequences of thinking in images are given a slightly different slant in the story "The Prophet" (*Prorok*) (1929). Here the burden of an overactive imagination is explicitly linked with sickness. Olesha's story is an interesting echo of Chekhov's *Ward No. 6*, where Gromov's acute sensitivity to the plight of others leads him to lose his mind at the sight of a prisoner in chains. In "The Prophet" Kozlenkov is overwhelmed by compassion when he hears the story of a girl who has hanged herself, and he resolves to perform a miracle and save her. He begins to interpret the ordinary behavior of others, and even natural phenomena such as a breeze, as confirmation of his special calling to do something miraculous. He sees an angel and a shepherd in his dreams and develops messianic delusions. In this story the suspension of the rules of ordinary life takes place involuntarily and leads to a world that appears to be governed by new laws but is actually nothing more than a state of delirium. While on the way to the hospital to perform his deed of healing, Kozlenkov suddenly realizes that he cannot continue, and, without motivation, he stops and turns back. In "Love," Shuvalov exercises a degree of control over his two worlds but in "The Prophet," Kozlenkov's entry into and exit from the realm of acute images and suspended rules takes place capriciously and without the apparent conscious participation of the character.

Yet, it would be wrong to attribute an overly dark or pessimistic meaning to the story, simply because the character appears unable to exercise control over his destiny. When he realizes that he cannot perform a miracle, Kozlenkov returns home to his dreams. This time the appearance of an angel evokes no special response in him. He merely awakes from his dream, takes a drink of water, chuckles to himself, and goes back to sleep, evidently unharmed by his brush with the world beyond the everyday. Kozlenkov's chuckle gives the conclusion to the story an enigmatic quality. Olesha is at his best, as in "The Prophet," when he preserves a Chekhovian ambivalence and ambiguity. In some of his other stories, particularly the later ones, the more explicit and programmatic Olesha becomes in the exposition of his themes, the less he appeals to the artistic sensibilities he is so assiduous in portraying and cultivating.

In "The Cherry Stone" the dreamer-narrator journeys in an unseen land where he sees the world differently, almost as a child for the first time. He asks rhetorically, "So does that mean that in defiance of everyone, in defiance of order and society, I create a world that does not obey any laws except the phantasmal laws of my own sensations?" (215). More so than Shuvalov, the narrator of "The Cherry Stone" deliberately fashions a world for himself with laws that are different from those of the real world. And, more than Shuvalov or Kozlenkov, he is conscious of the discrepancy between the real world and the solipsistic world of his own making.

The narrator of "The Cherry Stone" also has a double in the person of Avel', the down-to-earth party man, who knows about such things as five-year plans and who acts as a foil to the narrator's imaginative whimsies. Elizabeth Beaujour has noted that the character of Avel' is based on the biblical Abel, who is a righteous man and the elect of God.[17] As Robert Russell has shown, this biblical analogy may be extended also to the character of Fedya, who resembles Cain in his role as a tiller of the soil. In addition, just as Cain brought his fruit of the ground to God and was rejected, so is Avel' rejected by the girl he loves, Natasha.[18] Like so many of Olesha's principal characters Fedya is clearly an outsider, if not an outcast.

Nevertheless, Olesha is not content merely to mirror the biblical source he alludes to, for the conclusion of his own story is full of irony. First of all, the seemingly prosaic Avel' turns out to have an imagination, when he declares that in the center of the huge concrete building there will be a garden. Furthermore, it is in this garden that the cherry stone Fedya has planted will grow into a tree.

"The Cherry Stone" contains one of Olesha's best treatments of the competition between the unseen world of imagination with its solipsistically determined rules and the seen world of Soviet socialism. Olesha creates an especially sharp juxtaposition between these two worlds. The narrator's whimsical notions, such as the planting of the cherry stone given to him by Natasha, a girl who has spurned his love, would appear to form an irreconcilable conflict with the concrete world of five-year plans. Having established this apparently unbridgeable gap, Olesha proceeds in his best paradoxicalist fashion to introduce the possibility of an eventual union of the unseen world of imagination and the world of five-year plans. The cherry tree will grow in the garden of the new concrete edifice. Thus, the conclusion of "The Cherry Stone" is one of the most optimistic of Olesha's early works, and in this respect differs sharply from *Envy,* where there appears to be no such possible reconciliation between the world of imagination and the world of concrete.

In Olesha's short works a carnivalistic attitude toward life is manifested in certain stories, such as "Love," "The Cherry Stone," and "The Prophet" in the characters' experience of a world with rules that differ from the commonplace. In all of these stories, as in virtually all of Olesha's works, the summery setting contributes to a holiday atmosphere in which the characters and narrators are free to go for walks in parks and examine caterpillars, tree trunks, and little stalks of plants. The workaday life of the outside world exists, if at all, on the fringes of the characters' consciousness. This workaday world is often only alluded to symbolically, as in "The Cherry Stone," where the concrete colossus stands for the whole system of five-year plans.

The story *Al'debaran* (1931) is one of the few works by Olesha in which the characters are actually shown on the job. Here Tsvibol is described while working on a bulldozer. Yet, even despite the victory of the younger generation of doers and builders in this story, the predominant atmosphere is one of a lazy holiday. Olesha conveys this atmosphere both subtly and effectively in his image of the cloud with a big forehead (*lobastaya tucha*) that "turned his back, looked over his shoulder, and began to fall on its back" (244).

In some of his *ocherks* Olesha deals with subject matter that in other places is at the basis of his carnivalistic depiction of life. In these sketches, however, a truly carnivalistic spirit is not fully realized, even though the events or places described have a dramatically spectacular aspect. Two sketches, "At the Circus" (*V tsirke*) (1928) and "Spectacles" (*Zrelishcha*) (1937), are good examples of the way in which Olesha continually returns to certain favorite themes, in this case, the theme of the circus, and shows them from different perspectives.

In "At the Circus" Olesha finds that the contemporary circus is rather prosaic by comparison with the old circus: "If the ancient tightrope walker symbolized flight from prison or a journey into the window of one's lover, then the tightrope walker of the new circus portrays a city person, a coward, who has landed on a rope stretched out by a laundress" (208). And the clown, who used to cry, sing, and be scandalous, is now an uncertain figure. There are, however, some consolations for the modern circus-goer. One of these is the Chaplinesque figure that has replaced the traditional clown. He has the look of a typical city dweller, but under his sportcoat is hidden the fit, muscular physique of a sportsman. Olesha finds in this a suggestion to the urban spectators that they too could acquire such a physique if they were to train a bit. Even in his deceptive, urban garb, the Chaplin of the new circus is able to perform acrobatic feats that defy the laws of physics. It is exactly this play with the laws of physics, exemplified by the tightrope walker and the acrobats, that draws Olesha to the circus.

Olesha's description of the motorcycle in "Spectacles" is more inspired and more convincing than his lament about the passing of the old circus traditions in "At the Circus." He is particularly struck by the motorcycle riders, who ride up and down the sides of a special metal cage: "In the spectacle of a person moving vertically is an element of the strongest fantasy that is accessible to our consciousness. Such events comprise the limit of the fantastic. They are the most extraordinary for our earthly perception, because when they take place, for a second a picture arises before us of some nonexistent world with physical laws that are opposed to our own" (276).

While in some of his other sketches from 1936, a particularly productive year for Olesha, he appears to be almost blasé, in "Spectacles" he is invigorated and alive. In describing the circus, the motorcycles, and their drivers, he is clearly on his own turf. In his portrait the circus has the power to give one a fleeting look into a carnivalistic world, where the laws of physics and the rules of life are different from the everyday.

Two other sketches treat subjects that also would appear to lend themselves well to Olesha's love of the spectacular: "The Stadium in Odessa" (*Stadion v Odesse*) and "The First of May" (*Pervoe Maia*), both written in 1936. In "The First of May" Olesha concludes a short series of microsketches with a description of the May Day Parade in Odessa: "The procession lasts four hours. Since last year the May Day demonstrations have acquired a novelty: a carnival spirit. There are a lot of theater costumes, masks, wigs, cardboard noses, multi-colored feathers, and ribbons" (262).

Olesha hastens to note, however, that the participants in the parade have not really lost their seriousness and that they actually show disdain for their outlandish costumes. Thus, at the conclusion of "The First of May" he inadvertently produces something close to self-parody. For this is not a true carnival, but rather a description of an ersatz, trumped-up carnival in which the participants are unable even for a short time to act out their carnivalistic roles convincingly. Here his characteristic laconic style backfires on him. Instead of transmitting a feeling of movement or enthusiasm, a phrase such as "the procession lasts four hours" suggests the perfunctory style of a guidebook or a technical description. "The First of May" reflects Olesha's long-term fascination with spectacular events, but only in a feeble, almost distorted form. Rather than transforming a festive event into a carnivalistic one, as he does in his best work, here he brings it down to a mundane, prosaic level.

Virtually the same thing occurs in another of Olesha's sketches from 1936, "The Flight" (*Polet*), which is part of a brief trilogy called "Three Stories" (*Tri rasskaza*). At first glance one might think that such a subject would elicit in him a stimulating description of the fantastic nature of flight, or perhaps some suggestion of the ways in which flight reflects man's attempt to take the laws of physics to their limit. Instead, his technique of understatement leaves the reader completely nonplussed and never rises above the level of banalities: "I will never forget everything that comprised that flight. They are all marvelous things—the strict, business-like, masculine world. You want to return to it. A person who has completed a long flight begins to respect himself. He experiences a feeling of triumph" (271).

"The Stadium in Odessa," like "The First of May" and "The Flight," has a potentially spectacular subject. A stadium is the site of the most dramatic moments in both the novel *Envy* and in the play *A Conspiracy of Feelings*. And the soccer field is the subject of some of Olesha's best lyrical passages in *No Day without a Line*. Olesha begins this sketch with an historical overview of Odessa that includes references to Pushkin, Tolstoy, and the revolution of 1905. The climax occurs when the narrator arrives at the stadium and observes:

> You can't imagine a more marvelous spectacle.
> The knack for similes turns out to be powerless. What does it resemble? I don't know. I have never seen it before. It's a picture of the future.
> No, that's not so. It is exactly the border, the transition, the realized moment of transition from the present into the future.
> The green football field. We look from afar, from above. What purity and depth this green color has. You want to determine where the optical effect comes from. Where does such transparency and clarity come from? We don't have a telescope in our hands, there are no lenses before our eyes. (258)

"The Stadium in Odessa" concludes with a hymn in praise of the "government, the land of socialism, our homeland, her style, her beauty, her everyday, and her marvelous realities" (258). The hyperbolic evocation of the stadium thus turns out to be little more than the groundwork for this hymn. One might conclude that in the perilous year of 1936 Olesha knew just the right phrases to use, just the right notes to play. From an artistic point of view, however, it is not so much what this sketch and some of the others from 1936 contain but what is left out that is striking.

In many of his sketches from the middle of the 1930s Olesha is revisiting his old haunts, in both a literal and a literary sense. He is revisiting various festive occasions. He sees them from a great height and tells us how beautiful and optically interesting they are. Yet, his description of the stadium in Odessa is the epitome of what is lacking. The reader has been invited to a spectacle, but when the reader arrives, there are no performers, no event, only an empty structure. There is only simile—a good one, no doubt, because Olesha's eye is still sharp and he is still able to produce splashes of startling imagery. But the problem is that we have seen all of this, or something very like it, before and in more compelling circumstances. In this respect Olesha is a victim of his own past successes. The green soccer field of *Envy* is infinitely more interesting than the one in "The Stadium in Odessa" because in the former work it is the scene of dramatic interaction between characters and it is symbolically linked with their youthful aspirations.

The trouble with many of Olesha's sketches and some of his later stories is not that they are poorly crafted in and of themselves, but that they are only pale reflections of other accomplishments of a higher order. In "My Friend" (*Moi znakomyi*) the narrator exclaims about his friend, who is a follower of European fashion and is caught up in a cult of sport, hygiene, and comfort: "Oh, I simply envy him!" (233). Or, in "A Talk in the Park" (*Razgovor v parke*) (1933), Olesha proclaims, "Sport! I saw how it began." He is struck by the way in which racing cars leave "sky-blue whiskers of smoke" on the bushes when they disappear around a corner (255). All of these exclamations are genuine, and all of these images are arresting in their own way. Yet, they are not especially moving, because Olesha has already portrayed the essence of envy and evoked the spectacular nature of sport in a much more convincing fashion in *Envy*.

What appears to have happened in some of Olesha's sketches from 1936, such as "The First of May," "The Flight," and "The Stadium in Odessa," is that his strong need to rebel against usual conventions and expectations has finally resulted in a kind of rebellion against his own past practices and poetics. Thus, where in other places Olesha elevates potentially spectacular or even carnivalistic events, in these sketches he deflates them with his businesslike style and understatement. Perhaps "Spectacles" (1937) is something of an exception to this trend, since although the sketch is understated, it nevertheless creates the sort of impression its title suggests. In a short story, "Natasha" (1936), Olesha treats favorite themes, in this case sport and the relations between the generations, with some vigor and originality. An elderly professor discovers at the end that one of the young people he has been watching jump with parachutes is actually his daughter, Natasha, who had told him she was going to meetings.

Subsequently, many of Olesha's most characteristic themes and motifs appear in his stories, if at all, in an almost jaded aspect. For example, in 1945 Olesha wrote a story called "The Mirror" (*Zerkal'tse*) about a young Russian woman who has lost a mirror in which she can see the image of her lover, who has gone off to war. Eventually a Turkoman, whose singing the woman greatly admires, finds the mirror and returns it to her. For readers familiar with Olesha's play with mirrors and other aspects of visual perspective in *Envy* and his stories, the mirror in this story is a motif that appears to have grown flat and dull.[19] So too do Olesha's carnivalistic and spectacular depiction of and attitude toward life appear to have grown old and withered and have eventually died out. Before this process had completed itself, however, there took place several flashes of carnivalistic sensibility in Olesha's drama that illuminate not only his plays but the overall significance of the carnival in his work.

The Carnival on Stage

One might think that the stage and the screen would serve as fertile grounds for the carnivalistic depiction of life that pervades so much of Olesha's prose. And indeed, there are some plays and parts of plays where the ambience of the carnival is perceptible. Yet, overall, Olesha's drama is not nearly so suffused with the spirit of the carnival as are his novels and short stories. For instance, in *A List of Blessings*, the heroine Goncharova is asked to play the flute out of her backside, a scene that flouts conventional taste and morality with its vulgar implications in the same way that the carnival encourages the breaking of the usual moral codes and the presence of profanity and vulgarity not usually permitted.[20] The carnival spirit of profanation characteristic of this scene is not, however, sustained throughout the course of the play, except perhaps in a much weaker form in the emigré Tatarov's blasphemies about the Soviet Union.

One other echo of the carnival should be noted. It is related to the image of Charlie Chaplin which so captivated Olesha over the years. In *A List of Blessings* Goncharova sees a poor, unemployed man who looks like Charlie Chaplin. Within the image of Chaplin as Olesha portrays and perceives it, there is contained not only the poor, lonely, ugly man but also his double, who is rich, famous, and handsome. As Goncharova says, the theme of Chaplin is that of a "freak who wants to be beautiful, a beggar who wants to be wealthy" (P 111). In Olesha's story either the beggar is juxtaposed with his rich double or he himself wants to become a rich man. This double image of beggar/rich man has its basis in a carnivalistic perception of life. In the carnival the poor man is on an equal footing with the rich man and therefore becomes for a time one with his opposite. In Olesha there is no thought of a beggar's consciously earning the status he aspires to.

Writing on the traditional treatment of money in drama and literature, Olesha notes that "the dream of suddenly becoming wealthy was transformed into the captivating images of Cinderella and the ugly duckling."[21] In *A List of Blessings* Charlie Chaplin is explicitly treated as a kind of modern version of the ugly duckling. For Olesha the transformation from poor to rich takes place by a leap of the imagination, a carnivalistic imagination that sees no barriers between classes or groups. Olesha's unconscious attraction to the carnival and its imagery and his conscious fascination with its progenitor, European culture, nourish each other mutually. It is appropriate, therefore, that the image of Chaplin in the Europe of *A List of Blessings* should be that of a descendant of a carnival double.

In both *A Conspiracy of Feelings* and *Three Fat Men* pervasive eccentricity in the characters' behavior is one of the principal carnivalistic ingredients. In the dramatic version of *Three Fat Men* the role of Doctor Gaspar Arneri is expanded by comparison with the novel. Arneri's speech is loaded with unconscious irony and non sequiturs, and he becomes involved in all sorts of absurd situations. When Arneri loses his glasses he says, "You have to see a dream, and I see poorly without glasses" (P 211). Later, still without glasses, he gets his head stuck in a barrel.

Olesha skillfully amplifies the already heavily slapstick atmosphere of the novel in the stage version of *Three Fat Men*. In the play the balloon man also plays an enlarged role. The scene in which he is made into part of a cake the three fat men are about to eat for dessert is filled with riotous humor. In fact, the carnivalistic atmosphere that encompasses slapstick and other features of the novel yields to the hegemony of slapstick itself in the play. Nowhere else does Olesha employ so widely and so successfully such zany and nonsensical humor as in the play *Three Fat Men*.

Although *A Conspiracy of Feelings* displays in many places the ambience of the carnival that is found in *Envy*, the play is considerably different from the novel. The character of Andrei in the play has become more sympathetic, even sentimentalized, and less complex than in *Envy*.[22] He now reads Shakespeare and is, as Olesha calls him, the main hero of the play.[23] Kavalerov too is somewhat less complex, and he has been described by one critic as little more than an "envier."[24]

The character of Valya, who remains relatively undeveloped in *Envy*, comes to the fore in *A Conspiracy of Feelings*. In the play she is not the natural but the adopted daughter of Ivan. She is in love with Andrei, who at forty years of age is considerably older than she. Volodya Makarov, who is Valya's constant companion in *Envy*, has been left out of *A Conspiracy of Feelings* entirely. The soccer match, where Makarov comes into his own in *Envy*, never actually takes place in the play. The time immediately before the beginning of the game serves rather as the stage for the culmination of Ivan's and Kavalerov's plot to kill Andrei. At the end the soccer match begins just as the play comes to a close.

In *A Conspiracy of Feelings* Ivan Babichev's pillow symbolizes his eccentricity and his proclivity for living a life that is not simply out of the ordinary but often beyond the bounds of what is socially acceptable. First, Ivan incites Kavalerov to murder Andrei. He also makes a casual suggestion to a lover that he kill his mistress's husband. In addition to Kavalerov, Ivan's entourage consists of a motley assemblage of characters who come in comic, carnivalistic pairs. There are two older men, Mikhal Mikhalych and someone who is called simply "a respected old man," a woman and her daughter, two young men, and a pair of drunks, one very drunk and one less drunk. Ivan announces to his troupe, "I am your king. . . . I am king of the vulgarians" (P 73).

The whole gathering is conducted in a carnivalesque spirit that alternates between frivolity and scandal. Kavalerov suggests to Ivan that he show his troupe a miracle. Ivan consents, saying, "I agree to perform a miracle, but for that it is necessary that everyone in order tell his most cherished wishes" (P 74). The series of conventional wishes for property, love, and happiness that follows is broken by a candid remark of the less drunk guest: "You ask me what is your cherished wish, and I answer. I wish you, my neighbor Sergei Nikolaevich Mikulitsky, death. There it is! So that your room will be free" (P 77). This spirit of humorous scandal is continued when Mikhal Mikhalych expresses the wish that his wife, who is eight months pregnant, have a child who looks like him. Finally, Ivan dashes the hopes of his followers by telling them that he cannot fulfill their wishes, because "dead men can not wish. I am the king of the dead" (P 78). Ivan's remark may be understood figuratively in this context to mean that he is the leader of a group of people who are dead in the sense that their way of life and sensibilities are outmoded and about to be replaced. The feelings they possess, such as vanity, love, and cruelness, are also fated to perish because of the new social order being constructed by people like Andrei Babichev.

It is most likely that the notion of Ivan as the king of the dead comes from the drafts of *Envy* that contain a description of a group of corpses, including murderers, who were to have a parade to celebrate the old feelings in a truly carnivalistic fashion.[25] In *A Conspiracy of Feelings* Olesha stops short of incorporating the scene of dead men and women and uses instead Ivan's ragged company of people whose wishes and feelings are doomed. While including corpses in *Envy* might well have turned out to be a master stroke, their inclusion in *A Conspiracy of Feelings* would likely have gone beyond the imaginative scope of the play, which is generally more down to earth and less permeated by fantasy than the novel.

At the end of the fifth scene of *A Conspiracy of Feelings* Kavalerov has a crisis dream in which Valya and Andrei come to see him and in which he is discrowned in a thoroughly carnivalistic fashion. As will soon be evident, this dream has important consequences for the outcome of the play and its whole meaning. It is in this dream that Valya reprimands Andrei for not saying the kinds of poetic things Kavalerov says to her. What begins as an unmasking of Andrei, the king of sausages, is reversed when a doctor enters to give an examination of Kavalerov, Ivan's jester. Andrei actually helps the doctor "expose" Kavalerov by taking off his shirt. Here is what the doctor discovers:

> There . . . there . . . just a minute . . . the muscles . . . there . . . the musculature is flabby . . . there. . . . Lascivious, obviously lascivious . . . show your eyes. Let's see, let's see how they react. . . . He's insane! (P 70).

The discrowning of Kavalerov that takes place in *A Conspiracy of Feelings* in a dream is a parallel to the scene in *Envy* where Kavalerov is unmasked in front of the public at the soccer match by his inability to react to a soccer ball that lands at his feet in the stands. In *A Conspiracy of Feelings* the originality of Kavalerov's discrowning dream inheres in its outlandish comicality that is highlighted by the doctor's comments.

It is interesting that the doctor's examination, comic as it is, strikes at the heart of all of Kavalerov's major pretensions. His physical strength, which would be necessary in order to carry out the murder of Andrei, is shown to be inadequate. His romantic aspirations for Valya are exposed as nothing more than lewdness. Finally, his mind, the source of his rich imagination, is revealed to be deranged.

There are two endings to *A Conspiracy of Feelings*. In the original ending Kavalerov turns on Ivan and kills him instead of Andrei as a symbolic way of killing his past. The version of the play published in Olesha's *P'esy* in 1968 eliminates any killing whatsoever: when Kavalerov catches sight of Valya, he puts down his razor and is unable to raise it against his intended victim, Andrei. At the end Ivan orders Kavalerov to be taken away to a museum, Andrei orders them both to be taken away, and the soccer match begins (P 88–89). The question naturally arises as to which of the two endings is more consistent with what goes before it in *A Conspiracy of Feelings*

First, Kavalerov is a dreamer and a fantast but not a murderer. He lacks both the vigor and the initiative to commit murder. His envy of Andrei Babichev is far too irresolute to result persuasively in murder. Murdering either Andrei or Ivan is not only out of character for Kavalerov but also out of keeping with the play's carnivalistic spirit, because in the carnival there is symbolic killing but not real killing. Furthermore, it is Ivan and Kavalerov who play the role of jester-kings. Consequently, it is they and not Andrei who should be discrowned. Since Olesha has already anticipated the ultimate discrowning of Kavalerov in the dream scene with Andrei, Valya, and the doctor, the second ending of the play, in which Kavalerov fails to kill Andrei, becomes all the more persuasive. For this dream acts to foreshadow the ultimate unmasking of Ivan and Kavalerov and their plans to commit a senseless murder.

One observer claims that not only may *A Conspiracy of Feelings* be considered as a work that is separate from *Envy* but that the play is both "broader and stronger" than the novel.[26] The realignment and reinterpretation of characters in the play does in fact make it a substantially different work from the novel. Whether it is more successful as a work of literature, however, is doubtful. Certainly the play is more tidy in its structure, and its action unfolds at a greater pace and along a plot line more easily followed.

The same may be said about Olesha's dramatization of *Three Fat Men* by comparison with the novel. Yet, in *Envy*, the back and forth and sideways movement of the plot creates room for the novel's distinctive imaginative qualities and carnivalistic illogicality. Furthermore, the simplification of the major characters does not particularly enhance the play by comparison with the novel. If we suspend for a moment the contradiction inherent in comparing a play with a novel, we will certainly conclude that although *A Conspiracy of Feelings* is both a competent and interesting work in its own right, it is not of the same order of artistic accomplishment as *Envy*. The novel is in fact broader in its imaginative range, more provocative in its presentation of theme and character, and richer in almost all of its aspects.

The Epitome of the Carnival

It has already been suggested here that *Envy* is a special kind of metafiction that defies attempts at easy categorization and challenges certain preconceptions about novelistic structure. It remains to be shown what exactly holds the motley fabric of this novel together. By examining the novel as a work of carnivalistic literature it is possible to demonstrate that many of the novel's aspects that have usually been treated independently of one another comprise an organically integrated artistic whole. With this perspective it is also possible to elucidate the pivotal role of the soccer match, a role that has been largely ignored by the extensive criticism on the novel.[27]

The extent to which Olesha's *Envy* embodies not only many of the specific features and images but also the overall atmosphere of the carnival is striking. For the whole logic of *Envy*'s development, its view of the world, its treatment of character, and its predominant atmosphere are so profoundly permeated with the spirit

of the carnival that the novel is not only Olesha's most richly carnivalistic work but also a special exemplar of carnivalistic fiction
in twentieth-century Russian fiction.

The cornerstone of *Envy*'s carnivalistic ambience is its
pervasive eccentricity. This eccentricity is exemplified primarily,
but not solely, in the behavior of the two major characters, Ivan
Babichev and Kavalerov, who live a life which is both inside out
and out of the rut. With Ivan and Kavalerov eccentricity covers a
range from such whimsical acts as Kavalerov's throwing an egg at
a street sign and Ivan's peeping into other people's windows and
going up other people's stairways to their fundamental relationships with other people. Certainly the most visible sign of Ivan's
eccentricity is the yellow pillow which he carries about with him
on the streets of Moscow. This pillow is more than just a symbol
of the domesticity of which Ivan fancies himself the defender, for
it is also a symbol of the upside-down, inside-out world that he in-
habits. In the carnival clothes were often worn backwards or inside out, and various household utensils were worn as hats or
even used as weapons.[28]

When telling his "Tale about the Meeting of Two Brothers,"
which is itself filled with the carnival imagery of an
incongruously complected crowd and a clown in a monkey suit,
Ivan claims that he is "king of the pillows" and that "the pillow is
our coat of arms. Our banner. Shots get stuck in a pillow. We will
suffocate you with it" (77). Ivan's threat to use his pillow as a
weapon brings to mind the carnival custom of using household
utensils as mock weapons and thus gives his brand of eccentricity
a particularly carnivalistic flavor.

Olesha underscores the eccentricity of Ivan and Kavalerov in
an artistically brilliant manner by having them meet for the first
time (they have seen each other before, but not actually met) in
front of a mirror, because in front of a mirror is where "Unprecedented changes have taken place with the world, with the
rules of the world. . . . Here is a secret world where everything is
repeated with that stereoscopy and brightness that are subject
only to the distancing lenses of binoculars. . . . So sudden is the
destruction of the rules, so improbable is the change in proportions . . . everything has been destroyed, has changed and acquired a new order of rules [*pvavil'nost'*] . . . The greenery is too
green, the sky is too blue" (48–49). This is a statement of the carnivalistic situation that obtains in *Envy* where the old rules have

been thrown out and replaced by a new set of rules, and where, particularly for Ivan and Kavalerov, what is not normally acceptable or permitted in everyday life becomes the norm. It is particularly interesting that Olesha's much-remarked interest in optical perspective is the vehicle for this carnivalization of the order of rules. In the mirror or through the distancing lenses of binoculars the summer colors of *Envy's* setting, green and blue, are made more acute. Indeed, Olesha's fascination with the juxtaposition between closeup views and faraway ones is in the spirit of the carnival, where things and people appear in either enlarged or miniaturized versions of each other. It is eminently appropriate, therefore, that Olesha's two main carnival, parodic doubles, Ivan and Kavalerov, should begin their sojourn together in front of a mirror. When they leave the mirror after a considerable interval, "the two comics already were walking together. One a little shorter and a little thinner outdistanced the stride of the other" (63)—nothing less than the image of carnival doubles, who resemble each other in their roles as jesters but contrast in their height and girth.

One of the most important manifestations of Ivan's and Kavalerov's eccentricity is their love of verbal haranguing, indecent suggestions, and generally blasphemous remarks. Such behavior, which would be considered typical for the carnival, may acquire scandalous overtones when performed in an everyday situation. Ivan and Kavalerov have a penchant for creating scandalous public scenes. For example, Kavalerov insults Andrei Babichev, the man who rescued him from the gutters of the street, by calling him a sausage maker (*kolbasnik*) in public at the airshow (35). Ivan creates a similar confrontation with Andrei when he stops Andrei's car on a public street in order to berate him (60). Ivan and Kavalerov go beyond merely unconventional or scandalous taunting when they threaten several times to kill Andrei. In his rage Ivan threatens to strangle his own daughter, Valya, so that Volodya Makarov will not be able to win her. Even these death threats have a parallel in the cry "death to you" (*smert' tebe*) which people called out to each other during the carnival.[29]

In addition to various threats and insults, Kavalerov does not hesitate to make indecent suggestions about Andrei, for instance, when he accuses Andrei of sleeping with his niece, Valya, both in a letter (39) and in a conversation with Volodya (43). While such insinuations would be considered acceptable in the carnival and are symptomatic of Kavalerov's typically carnivalistic behavior and attitude toward life, they are clearly beyond the bounds of decency in everyday life. Throughout *Envy* Kavalerov and Ivan are consistently provocative and scandalous in their behavior, both in private and in public.

Ivan and Kavalerov are not the only characters who form a carnivalistic, parodic pair. Relationships between characters in *Envy*, despite the fact that they are often characterized primarily as a conflict between the older and the younger generations or as a battle between positive and negative characters, are rather complex and varied. One of the most graphic ways in which Olesha creates this complicated system of character relationships is through a network of parodic doubles reminiscent of the carnival. And just as in the carnival, where there is familiar contact between all kinds and classes of people, some of the contrasts found in the pairings in *Envy* may have surprising or humorous implications.

Each pair contains within itself both points of contrast and points of similarity, that is, two characters may share basic characteristics but in different proportions. For instance, while Andrei and Ivan share certain personality and physical traits, each expresses them in a different fashion. The chubby Ivan is a kind of scaled-down version of Andrei. Each is concerned with family life, but, while Ivan wants to preserve it as it is, Andrei wants to remake it. Both are builders: Andrei is involved in the construction of a prosaic communal dining hall, whereas Ivan is the creator of the fantastic, imaginary Ophelia. Ophelia in her turn is a kind of unexpected obverse parodic double or mirror image of Volodya in that she is a machine with human qualities, whereas Volodya is a man who is trying to acquire the characteristics of a machine. Perhaps the most humorous parodic pair is that of Andrei and Anechka Prokopovicha, who have a number of things in common. They both display a mothering instinct, which leads them to pick up waifs, such as Kavalerov, off of the street. Andrei has an even more obvious feminine quality: he is so plump that when he runs his breasts bounce. Finally, Andrei and Anechka are paired with one another through their association with sausages: Andrei makes sausages, and Anechka looks like one.

The relationships between characters are further complicated and enriched by the fact that the prevalent images of each of the major adult characters in *Envy*, Andrei, Ivan, and Kavalerov, have definite affinities with typical carnival figures. The rotund Andrei, glutton and sausage maker, evokes the image of the figure of Carnival himself, "who usually took the form of a fat man, pot-bellied, ruddy, cheerful, often hung about with eatables (sausages, fowl, rabbits), seated on a barrel or accompanied by a cauldron of macaroni."[30] Ivan and Kavalerov are frequently portrayed as clowns, jesters, or comics. Kavalerov actually calls himself Andrei's jester, and for a time he plays this role by running errands for Andrei and entertaining him in the evenings. At the same time, as befits double characters who are not only juxtaposed to each other, but are internally ambivalent, Ivan and Kavalerov have the image of pretender or imposter kings who threaten figuratively to unseat Andrei. Ivan is also the self-proclaimed king of pillows and vulgarians.

The gluttony associated with several of the characters forms a leitmotif in *Envy* that was one of the most important themes of the carnival as it was practiced in early modern Europe.[31] In addition to their preoccupations with consuming and making food the characters' overindulgence takes the form of habitual drunkenness, especially for Ivan and Kavalerov. Throughout *Envy* Ivan and Kavalerov engage in a kind of movable drinking bout, as they spend most of their time in taverns and beer halls. Shortly after he meets Kavalerov, Ivan makes an explicit statement of his carnivalistic attitude when he invites Kavalerov to join him in celebrating the end of the old era by "creating a scandal" and "going out with a bang" (65). Ivan's consciously carnivalistic attitude toward life helps to impart to *Envy* the atmosphere of a kind of Mardi Gras celebration on the threshold between the old and new eras.

Ivan's conduct of his conspiracy of feelings in his role as king of the vulgarians has a number of striking affinities with the imagery of the carnival. His self-made coronation is performed in the manner of the crowning of the jester-king of the carnival:

He allowed himself to climb up on a table. . . . Awkward and in no way prepared for such tricks, he climbed over heads, grasping at palm leaves; bottles broke, the palm plunged. He got established on the table, and waving two empty mugs like dumb-bells, began to shout:
Here I stand on the heights, surveying a swarming army. To me! To me! Great is my host! Little actors dreaming of glory.

Unhappy lovers! Old maids! Accountants! Men of Ambition! Fools! Knights! Cowards! To me! Your king has come, Ivan Babichev! (57)

The host Ivan urges to follow him consists of just the sort of mésalliances that give Ivan's imagination and consequently *Envy* itself a distinctive carnivalistic sensibility. Ivan's reign as carnival king is short lived, however, and when he calls for a keg of beer to toast great events, he and his company are thrown out into the street. This is only Ivan's first discrowning. The second takes place when he is called in by the GPU for questioning.

In the drafts to *Envy* Olesha had contemplated a bold climax to Ivan's conspiracy of feelings—a parade in which representatives of human emotions who had come back from the dead would take part in the celebration of Ivan's unveiling of Ophelia at the opening of Chetvertak. This parade was apparently to have been a part of Kavalerov's hallucinations in the next to last chapter of the novel.[32] In this scene Kavalerov is dressed in a blanket:

"A blanket! everyone exclaimed. "What a marvelous blanket, how good it would be to sleep under such a blanket. . . .
"With a lover!"
"With a beautiful girl!"
/. . ./ "The chosen one! What a blanket he has!"
"It is blooming, like a meadow!"
"Bravo! Bravo! Bravo!"

Ivan proclaims that "this is my host" and greets the entourage:

Young men kissed the girls on the shoulders. They held in their hands a woman with blue cheeks and neck. Kavalerov guessed, "Ach, it is /. . ./ a casualty of sulfuric acid, a casualty of jealousy. A thin youth looked out of a window, waving /. . ./ the end of a rope around his neck. Ach, he's the one who hanged himself /. . ./ out of unhappy love! A jockey /. . ./ in a light blue outfit, tossed his cap. "Ach, it's the famous jockey . . . glory. . . /. . ./ Someone all disheveled /. . ./ broke through the crowd. His hands were covered with blood. /. . ./ They applauded in the crowd. Ach, it's a murderer! /. . ./

Greeting! Greetings! /. . ./
They made an inspection. /. . ./ They went around the for-
mation.
"Who are you?" /. . ./ asked Ivan, stopping first before one,
and then before another.
"I am a fool," answered one. /. . ./
"I am a glutton."
"And you!"
"I am a wanton."
"I am a cheerful fellow:"
"And you?"
"I am a stubborn man."
"I am a gossip:"
"And this . . ."
"Arrogance incarnate."
"And I am a coward:"
"Greetings! Greetings!"
"We are lovers!"
"We /. . ./ are sick at heart."
"/. . ./ And we are cruel!"
"/. . ./ And who is he?"
"An ambitious man:"
"And I am simply /. . ./ an honest merchant."[33]

After hundreds of different people go by Ivan says, "There is
the parade of human feelings. I am happy. Now we will go.
/. . ./ Ophelia is there!"[34] Kavalerov's garb, which consists of his
blanket, is an especially appropriate costume for him, since he
spends so much time either in a state of reverie or outright
delirium in bed. His blanket also gives him an eccentric, carnivalistic trademark to match Ivan's pillow. As Ingdahl notes,
this whole description of the parade of feelings is thoroughly
imbued with the spirit of the carnival and of carnivalized
literature. The erotic conversation of the participants in the
parade that is sparked by the sight of Kavalerov's blanket is
reminiscent of Dostoevsky's story "Bobok," in which corpses
who are lying in their graves also engage in scandalous, erotic
discussion among themselves. Certainly the major literary
predecessor of Olesha's portrayal of the parade of feelings in the
form of corpses is Goethe's description of Walpurgis night in
Faust.[35]

It should also be pointed out that the draft of the parade has an interesting point of contact with Bulgakov's description of Woland's ball in *The Master and Margarita* (*Master i Margarita*) (1966–67). Here Margarita presides over a procession of corpses, among whom murderers and suicides are also prominent. The placement of murderers and suicides in positions of the greatest respect, both in Olesha's draft and in Bulgakov's novel, is emblematic of the topsy-turvy world of the carnival, where everyday expectations do not apply or are explicitly overturned. In both places, mundane norms are suspended and give way to both uninhibited behavior and conversation.[36]

There are, of course, significant differences between Olesha's depiction of the last parade of feelings and Woland's ball in *The Master and Margarita*. Most important of these is the fact that in *Envy* the parade would have taken place only in the delirious fantasy of the sick and drunken Kavalerov. In Bulgakov's novel, on the other hand, Woland's ball takes place completely on the level of genuine, unmitigated fantasy. Nevertheless, had Olesha incorporated his cavalcade of corpses into the final version of *Envy*, he would have had the distinction of composing a precursor to Bulgakov's splendid creation, which has no real counterpart in Russian literature of the Soviet period. It would have also brought one of the major motifs of *Envy* to a spectacular climax and raised the novel to greater imaginative heights.

It is hard to say why Olesha decided not to use the parade of corpses in *Envy*, but it is possible that he lacked the confidence to attempt what would have been a daring and provocative stroke in his first major work. The cowards, fools, and petty merchants in the parade are the same kinds of people Ivan exhorts to join him in the beer hall. The introduction of murderers and suicides, even in the form of Kavalerov's delirium, however, would have given *Envy* a potentially more disturbing aspect. It would have created a sharp contrast between the little, ordinary people of Ivan's entourage and extraordinary ones who had gone beyond the law and thereby would have broadened the range of the novel's carnivalistic mésalliances. In any case, the draft of the parade that did not enter *Envy*'s final form provides striking and convincing proof of the profoundly carnivalistic manner in which Olesha conceives of the novel's atmosphere, the characters, and their behavior.

Before the soccer match it is really only Ivan and Kavalerov who have been shown as though living life in the carnival. The soccer match is the culmination of the carnivalistic motifs in *Envy*, because here all of the characters become caught up in one great carnivalistic event. Perhaps it is paradoxical to suggest that the soccer match is the climax of a novel that does not have a conventional plot or structure. To a large extent *Envy* moves back and forth and sideways but not forward toward an inexorable goal or conclusion. A number of narrative devices tend to break down any sense of forward progress. There is constant switching between what is ostensibly action and the musings, reflections, and recollections of the characters. Fantasy alternates with reality. Flashbacks are common; some of them are found in the form of letters, which together with other materials such as songs, notes, and signs that have been discussed here act to break up an already fragmented narrative.

All the same, there are definite principles and patterns on which *Envy* is constructed. The first of these is juxtaposition. On the most obvious level, part one, told in first-person narration from the point of view of Kavalerov, contrasts with part two, where third-person narration dominates, largely from Ivan's point of view. Furthermore there is a tendency in *Envy* for the major events, whether they take place on the plane of reality or the plane of fantasy, to occur in linked pairs. In virtually every case these events are characterized by the imagery of the carnival square in that they take place in a crowd of people, some of whose behavior is unusual, absurd, or scandalous. In this way Kavalerov's calling Andrei a sausage maker at the airshow is a direct parallel with Ivan's subsequent stopping of Andrei's car on the street. Also, Kavalerov's visit to Chetvertak, Andrei's communal dining hall, is a kind of artistic prelude to Ivan's imaginary "Tale of the Meeting of Two Brothers," which takes place in the structure's scaffolding.

Ivan's tale of the two brothers is worthy of special attention, because of its pronounced carnivalistic tenor. The crowd that assembles before Chetvertak contains a motley assortment of carnival mésalliances: a school boy, a ballerina, a clown, some actors, and Ophelia. The combination of these characters, the setting in the scaffolding, and Ivan's swinging on a rope suggest the performance of a kind of fantastic circus. Here the carnivalesque crowd brings to mind another of Ivan's fantasies, the army of people Ivan plans to lead as their king.

The various events in *Envy* that occur in parallel with each other, and in many instances reflect mutually on each other, are of course not the only elements of the novel that are based on contrast and juxtaposition. The several sets of parodic double characters and passages built on the juxtaposition of elevated versus naturalistic motifs, such as Ivan's philosophical discourses *de profundis* in beer halls, also complement the binary foundation of *Envy*'s structure. Such a binary structure is itself like that of the carnival, which consists of the oppositions between carnival and Lent, carnival and the everyday,[37] and crowning and discrowning of the carnival king. The scenes from Ivan's imagination and the other events in which he and Kavalerov actually participate are not in the strict sense foreshadowings of the soccer match. Nonetheless the imagery of the carnival square, carnival mésalliances, and eccentric behavior ally them with the soccer match as part of a series that has its epitome in the match, the novel's largest and most thoroughly carnivalistic event.

For all of *Envy*'s unconventionality in the realm of narrative technique, Olesha uses the old-fashioned, traditional device of direct foreshadowing in connection with the soccer match. This device is entirely appropriate, since as *Envy* suggests on many levels, neither the new nor the old can be perceived as such except in relation to one another. Olesha introduces the possibility of a soccer match relatively early in *Envy*, in the fifth chapter when Andrei tells Kavalerov that Volodya Makarov is a famous soccer player (21). Kavalerov later notes this fact in his letter to Babichev (38). Finally, near the end of the thirteenth chapter Makarov mentions in his own letter to Babichev that he will be playing for the combined Moscow team against the Germans (45). In the second part of *Envy* there is no mention of the soccer match until the seventh chapter, where Olesha provides an extensive artistic foreshadowing of the game that follows in the next two chapters. This foreshadowing, to borrow a term from sport, is literally and figuratively a "warm-up" for the match itself and is found in the passage where Kavalerov and Ivan observe Volodya and Valya playing in a small yard.

Olesha's technique of miniaturizing things—whether through the wrong end of binoculars or from a high vantage point—initiates this episode, in which Kavalerov first catches sight of Volodya and Valya through the small windows of a second-story gallery. Except for the absence of competition this

whole scene is actually a miniature of the match in that many of
the motifs and images found there are encountered here on a
small scale. The high vantage point from the gallery prefigures the
view from the stands of the stadium. The little yard, which is
"terribly green" (80), is simply a smaller version of the larger,
green field at the stadium. Volodya's and Valya's high-jumping
over an outstretched rope is an informal precursor to the game.
Finally, even the pose which Valya assumes in the yard, with her
legs spread wide apart, is exactly the same one she will take at
one point at the soccer match. Olesha's frequent use of parallel
structures, motifs, and events is also reflected in Ivan's reaction to
seeing Valya playing in the little yard. Prefiguring Kavalerov's
similar realization at the soccer match, Ivan comes to understand
here that Valya, in whom he had hoped to unite the best of both
the new and old worlds, is inaccessible to him: "I was wrong,
Valya . . . I thought that all feelings had perished, love and devo-
tion and tenderness, but everything has remained, Valya. Only
not for us, and for us there remains only envy and envy" (82). At
this point, however, Kavalerov is unwilling to accept the resigna-
tion of Ivan that "youth has passed" and that "the conspiracy of
feelings has failed," and he vows to kill Andrei at the soccer
match the next day.

It is here that Olesha finally makes explicit the previous implicit foreshadowings of the match. At the same time, he creates
the expectation that a main conflict of the novel, the one between
Kavalerov and Andrei, will be resolved in a dramatic fashion at
the game.

The soccer match in *Envy* occupies a special place in the novel
in a number of ways for a number of reasons. In order fully to ap-
preciate the role of the match it is helpful briefly to note the special cultural status of soccer in Russia in the 1920s. Soccer had already become the most popular sport in Russia, especially among
young people, even before World War I. During the 1920s soccer
was the primary sport in which the Soviets played international
matches. With specific reference to *Envy*, it is possible to assert
that the soccer match is unmistakably a reference to a match
played on 21 May 1927 between a combined Moscow side and a
combined team of players from a German workers' club called
"Saxony," won by Moscow 4 to 1.[38] The fact that it was the only
international match that the combined Moscow team played that
year makes the game special indeed. Furthermore, for at least a

number of contemporary Muscovite readers the game would conceivably have been the only event in *Envy* that clearly had its basis in a real, historical occurrence.

In *Envy*, a novel where so much takes place on the plane of fantasy, Olesha takes great pains to stress exactly the realism of the soccer match. He gives the reader a precise description of how the game is played: "Play continues for ninety minutes, with a short interval after forty-five minutes. After the interval the teams change ends of the field" (84). He follows this dry, factual description, which could serve in any rule book of the game, with an explanation of how the wind affects the course of play and which tactics the Moscow team employs in playing against it. In all of this explanation and the subsequent account of the game, there is clearly evident the eye of an expert. As we know, in his youth Olesha was in fact a skilled, avid soccer player whose life was for a time caught up in playing sport and soccer until he was discovered to have a weak heart.[39] Only after giving the reader the fundamentals of play, which he knew by rote, does Olesha proceed with the creation of the sort of imagery typical of *Envy*, such as the description of Makarov catching the ball and falling "in the form of a colored bomb" (85).

While the realism of the match is apparent, it is also by its very nature out of the ordinary. In his description of the game both before and during its course Olesha underlines just this extraordinarily festive and exceptional nature of the occasion: "They were excited by the anticipation of an *exceptional spectacle. . . .* Twenty thousand spectators packed the stadium. There was to be an *unprecedented holiday*—the long-awaited match between the Moscow and German teams" (83; italics added).

The behavior of the crowd and the whole atmosphere at the stadium is completely unrestrained, in the spirit of the carnival. The spectators "argued, shouted, and brawled over nothing" (83) in anticipation of the start of the match. Adding to the festive nature of the match is a brass band, which played at important matches at that time but which is drowned out by the roar of the crowd when the Soviet players come out onto the field and the "spectators fell against the railings and stamped their feet on the boards" (84).

The soccer match in *Envy* displays not only the generally carnivalistic atmosphere of life out of the rut, but also many of the principal events typical of the carnival. Although practice of the carnival throughout history varied from place to place and from era to era, there is a basic core or structure. Three elements that Peter Burke has described as central in the carnival of early modern Europe are a procession, a competition, and a play, usually a farce of some kind.[40] The only element missing in *Envy* is the play, but the game is after all, in a figurative sense, a special kind of drama itself, with respect to what takes place both on the field and in the stands. Before the start of the match the players come onto the field in a procession. The spectators shout the German star Getzke's name and are further enlivened by his novel, "foreign manner of greeting," which consists of shaking his clasped hands over his head. And, just as in the carnival, where the participants' costumes help to create a festive atmosphere, so here do the players' uniforms, which Olesha describes in detail. The Germans wore "orange, almost golden jerseys with greenish stripes on the right side of the breast and black shorts" (83). The Soviet team is in red shirts and white shorts.

These are not the only details of the players' appearance that Olesha focuses on. During the halftime the German players mix together with the Muscovites on the field, creating the sort of free association between disparate groups of people typical of the carnival. Up close the spectators can see the scratches on the players, the blades of grass on their rumpled uniforms, and even the way Getzke tends to a blow on his elbow. From high above the field in the stands, however, "everything produced a lighter, more festive impression" (87). Here as elsewhere Olesha creates a carnivalistic contrast between large and small scales through his juxtaposition of near and far perspectives.

Other important aspects of the carnival figure in the soccer match, if in a somewhat modified form. In Burke's characterization of the carnival it "was not only a festival of sex but a festival of aggression. . . . The violence, like the sex, was more or less sublimated into ritual. Verbal aggression was licensed."[41] At the stadium in *Envy* the sexual element is first manifested in a latent form in the crowd's and Kavalerov's attention to Valya: "They paid attention to the charming girl in the rose colored dress, almost a little girl, childlessly heedless of her poses and movements and in addition having such an appearance that everyone wanted to be noticed by her, as though she was a celebrity or the daughter of a famous person" (83). Valya's sexuality is revealed much more explicitly during the interval between the halves, when the wind blows her dress up around her face. Ritualized verbal aggression is exhibited in the shouting and arguing of the spectators. While outright violence as such plays no part in the match, ritualized violence and aggression are inherent features of soccer. There is also overt aggression in the play of Getzke, who is at once creative in making scoring opportunities and destructive in disrupting his team's overall plan of attack. The potential for violence lies not so much in the playing of the game as in Kavalerov's threat to kill Andrei Babichev.

As noted, the carnival is characterized in its essence by various paired oppositions such as carnival versus Lent and carnival versus everyday. In *Envy* the soccer match is the one real event most sharply juxtaposed with the everyday. The match, because of its strong affinity with the carnival, and because it is in its simplest form a contest between two opposing sides, is ideally suited to act as a vehicle for the summation or highlighting of the themes and motifs in a novel largely constructed out of various contrapuntal oppositions. The younger generation competes with the older. East opposes West in a number of levels, as Germans battle Russians, and Makarov the collectivist duels Getzke the individualist. Finally, Kavalerov is pitted against Andrei Babichev.

The failure of Kavalerov to carry out his promise to kill Andrei, as well as the failure of Ivan Babichev's conspiracy of feelings, has been ascribed to the two conspirators' understanding the "meanness of their revolt" when they see "the radiance of Valya."[42] This interpretation is persuasive with regard to Ivan, especially in light of the passage quoted earlier, in which he laments to Valya that love has remained but that for him there is only envy. And in Olesha's play, *A Conspiracy of Feelings*, it is clear that at the end of the play the sight of Valya prevents Kavalerov from killing Babichev with a razor.[43] Nevertheless, in *Envy* itself an incident that takes place at the soccer match before Kavalerov encounters Valya in the crowd has already spelled the defeat of Kavalerov's plan; it is the moment when the soccer ball lands at Kavalerov's feet:

The play stopped. The players froze caught unaware. The picture of the field, green and multi-colored, which had been moving the whole time, now stood stock still at once. . . . Kavalerov's spite grew stronger. Everyone was *laughing* around him. . . . At that moment all the thousands, as much as they could, presented Kavalerov with their unsolicited attention, and this attention was *laughable*. . . .

It is possible that Valya was *laughing* at him too, a man who had turned up under the ball. It is possible that she is doubly joyful, *mocking* an enemy in a *funny* situation. (86–87; italics added)

Finally, since Kavalerov is apparently paralyzed by his encounter with the ball, Andrei Babichev, who is sitting nearby and who does not even notice Kavalerov, calls for the ball and throws it back onto the field himself, trying hard to be serious in an inherently humorous position. Kavalerov's failure to pick up the ball, which contrasts with Babichev's aggressive response, shows him totally incapable of action and hence indicates the failure of his plan to kill Babichev. The reaction of the crowd, especially its laughter, precipitates a total discrowning of Kavalerov in the manner of the carnival. Bakhtin's characterization of Raskolnikov's dream about the old woman might apply equally to the image of Kavalerov and the ball: "Before us is the image of the carnival imposter-king being discrowned by the ridicule of the entire folk on the public square."[44]

The image of Kavalerov as a discrowned imposter king is particularly apt. Throughout *Envy* he contemplates or threatens various actions that would bring him the attention of the public and would demonstrate his power over other men. Specifically, he threatens more than once to do battle with or kill Andrei. The most aggressive act Kavalerov is able to muster, however, is to call Andrei a sausage maker at the airshow. Kavalerov's double, Ivan, also constantly conspires to destroy Andrei. He too imagines himself to be something he is not, namely, the leader of the last conspiracy of feelings and the king of the vulgarians. His means of destroying Andrei are in the end no more effective than Kavalerov's, for Ivan's scheme for Ophelia to wreck Andrei's Chetvertak turns out to be nothing more than an elaborate construction of fantasy.

Ivan has already in effect been discrowned as the self-styled king of the vulgarians, when he is taken away from his beer hall audience to the GPU. Kavalerov's discrowning is even more closely related to the tradition of the carnival. In particular, the crowd's laughter displays carnivalesque ambivalence, since it contains elements both of ridicule and simple rejoicing at a humorous situation. After he has been subjected to the ridicule of the crowd in the public square of the stadium, Kavalerov is rendered incapable of any subsequent action. Kavalerov and Ivan are shown then to be imposter carnival kings whose discrownings expose their illusions of power to be imaginative but unattainable fantasies.

Kavalerov's only remaining hope after his unmasking, and it is of course a vain one, is that Valya will somehow give her love to him. This is where the real significance of Kavalerov's last encounter with Valya lies, not in the failure of the plan to kill Andrei, which has already been crushed under the weight of the crowd's discrowning laughter.

Just before the second half begins, the wind, which has continued to blow throughout the match, gives Kavalerov one last chance to spy on Valya's "purity" and "tenderness" by blowing her dress up around her face. In her battle with the wind and her dress Valya accidentally comes up next to Kavalerov. It is here that he realizes that she is a "creature from another world, foreign and extraordinary," and he feels that her "purity is inaccessible—both because she was a young girl and because she loved Volodya—and how insoluble her seductiveness was" (88). He asks her to take pity on him, but she does not hear and walks away. Now that he has failed on every count, Kavalerov gets drunk and returns to Anechka Prokopovicha, who is the embodiment of his degradation.

While the failure of Kavalerov's dreams of power and love is highlighted, to an extent even brought about by the crowd at the stadium, it is compounded by the victory of Makarov. Makarov's victory here is not necessarily that of the winning side, although it is clear as the spectators suppose that Getzke's selfish play will demoralize the German team and that the Soviets will win in a rout.[45] The point is that Makarov's triumph is primarily an aesthetic one, regardless of the final outcome of the match. This is evident in Olesha's description of Makarov's play, as he makes one dazzling save after another: "Volodya did not catch the ball—he tore it from its line of flight, and as though violating physics, submitted to the action of indignant forces. He flew up together with the ball, spinning—screwing himself onto it exactly: he surrounded the ball with his whole body—with his knees, stomach, and chin, throwing his weight against the speed of the ball, the way they throw a rag to put out a flame" (84).

The critical reception of Volodya Makarov has been largely, almost universally negative. An early Soviet critic called him a "parodic figure," and a more recent American critic has described Makarov's sterility at length.[46] There is no doubt that Makarov's wish to become a machine, which ought to be perceived as more naive than serious, as well as his intention not to love Valya for four years, is hardly endearing stuff. On the other hand, it is remarkable that critics have ignored the extremely sympathetic portrayal of Volodya at the soccer match, the one time in the novel when he is performing the activity he does best and the moment when he is the main focus of attention. Olesha's admiration for Makarov is manifested not only in his description of his brilliance as a goalkeeper but also and more importantly in his assessment of Makarov's overall play and approach to the game. In addition to wanting terribly to win, Makarov worries about each of his teammates and is also interested in the impression the Soviet style of play is making on the German footballers: "As a soccer player, Volodya was the complete opposite of Getzke. Volodya was a professional sportsman—and the other was a professional player. For Volodya the general course of play, the general victory [obshchii khod igry, obshchaia pobeda], and the outcome were important—Getzke strove only to show his own skill" (85).

Critics who point out the ways in which Kavalerov and Ivan Babichev represent certain aspects of Olesha's own personality and outlook must also reckon with the fact that Makarov too stands for an important part of Olesha's youth.[47] In the intermission between halves, the spectators are so captivated with Makarov's play that they pick him up and throw him in the air (Kachali Volodiu Makarova) (87). It is extremely likely that there is an autobiographical basis for this occasion: the time that Olesha played his last soccer game and the schoolboys who had liked his play ran out onto the field after the game and threw him in the air (menia kachali).[48] It was after this match that Olesha was found to have a weak heart and was forbidden to play any more, so that it is obvious that the whole experience made a profound impression on him.

In Envy there are two reasons for the importance of this passage. First, having discrowned the old imposter carnival king, Kavalerov, the crowd now crowns Volodya the new king by its action. Second, it demonstrates not only the spectators' sympathy for Makarov but also Olesha's; like Makarov, Olesha is concerned with the general course of play and its aesthetic qualities. This concern should not be surprising, for Olesha's characters, including the secondary ones, are rarely one-sided. For example, the elusive quality of Valya, who like Volodya has been much maligned, is well illustrated by the fact that one critic has called her "earthy" while another believes that she is "ethereal."[49]

Just as Olesha previews the soccer match with the "warm-up" in the small, green yard, so does he follow it with a series of afterimages in the inebriated dreams of Kavalerov, who gets completely drunk after he leaves the stadium. Kavalerov's dream recapitulates several of the game's motifs in a fantastic and symbolic fashion. He sees a ball flying above the green, then himself flying above the crowd. Andrei, surrounded by people, stands at the top of a stairway embracing Volodya. Finally, borne by the music of the band, Valya, with her dress and ribbons flying, floats into Volodya's arms. At the end of Kavalerov's extended hallucinations (90–92), which include Ivan's destruction by Ophelia, he is left with the reality of sharing Anechka with the disillusioned Ivan. As the carnival must eventually yield to the everyday, so does the intoxicated carnival celebration of Ivan's and Kavalerov's dreams and fantasies give way to the everyday and the state of indifference to which they drink at the end of the novel (94).

It is tempting to conclude that the soccer match provides a clear-cut resolution of *Envy's* complex of juxtapositions and conflicts. Youth seems to win out over age. Both Andrei and Volodya defeat Kavalerov and Ivan. And the collectivist Makarov's victory over the selfish individualist Getzke seems assured in terms of both aesthetics and results. Yet, despite the best efforts of Makarov, Getzke scores a goal, and the crowd is captivated by his personality and play.[50] Furthermore, Olesha's ambivalence toward his characters and their own inherent ambivalence militate against placing them in the easy categories of winners and losers. In this respect *Envy* adheres to the spirit of the carnival, which is by its nature ambivalent and dualistic rather than didactic or prescriptive. Ivan and Kavalerov in particular vacillate between the poles of aggression and passivity. That this aggression never goes beyond the stage of verbal assault to outright violence is also in keeping with the tradition of the carnival, where there is mock violence but seldom real violence.

The different manifestations of the carnival principle that run throughout *Envy* integrate apparently unrelated aspects of the novel and give them artistic coherence. The typically carnivalistic contrasts between large and small find expression in Olesha's celebrated manipulations of optical perspective. The kaleidoscope of colors met in the novel—primarily green, blue, and yellow —suggests the myriad of colors encountered in the carnival. Ubiquitous images and evocations of spring, which are often connected with green grass, and the eccentric, giddy behavior of Olesha's carnival doubles combine to make *Envy* on one level a celebration of spring or an extended Shrovetide or spring carnival.

Envy is such a profoundly carnivalistic novel largely because its artistic view of the world is shaped along the lines of the sharp contrasts and contradictions, mockeries and vagaries, ups and downs, bums and big shots of which the carnival consisted. Moreover, Olesha portrays the era he describes in *Envy* in terms of one of the carnival's major themes and motive forces, namely, change and renewal. Near the end of the novel Olesha shows Kavalerov on the threshold of Anechka's apartment, and by extension on the threshold of a decision about himself. This passage is emblematic of the situation Olesha describes in *Envy*, that is, the world in the process of transformation and change on the threshold between two epochs. The disparate elements of character behavior, optical perspective, thematic exposition, atmosphere, and setting all resonate, either directly or indirectly, with features of the carnival, thus giving the novel, which at first glance seems so disjointed, a definite underlying poetic unity.

As we have seen, *No Day without a Line* helps retrospectively to illuminate certain aspects of *Envy*, particularly its structural properties. Working in the opposite direction, *Envy*, with its full-blown carnivalistic character and aesthetics, prospectively enables the reader to perceive the sometimes more subtle aspects of a carnivalistic sensibility that are manifest in Olesha's subsequent work. The variations on a carnivalistic attitude toward life that appear throughout Olesha's works highlight the many correspondences that obtain among them, some of which are unexpected. For example, the carnivalistic settings, mésalliances, and eccentricities of both *Envy* and *Three Fat Men*, together with the several motifs they have in common, form a surprising number of significant links between these two works that are otherwise so apparently different from one another. In addition, the many leitmotifs of carnival underline one of the salient features of Olesha's works when considered as a whole: they display a perceptible fondness for constantly rearranging and reexamining a fairly stable body of themes, character types, and motifs in different contexts and from different points of view. The many interconnections and parallels between *Envy* and Olesha's early stories are a primary example of this phenomenon. Olesha's repertoire of narrative techniques comprises a similar pattern in that it too is comprised largely of a series of variations on a basic structure that may be found in most of what Olesha wrote.

3 /
The Poetics of Dialogue

OLESHA's best works are so thoroughly dialogical because dialogue takes place in them on a number of different levels. One of the most important of these is the level of narrative structure. For the word in an artistic text to be perceived as dialogical rather than monological, it must, of course, be addressed to another person, either implicitly or explicitly. Dostoevsky's *Notes from Underground* (*Zapiski iz-pod polia*) (1864) is certainly one of the most graphic examples of a dialogical narrative. Here virtually every word of the underground man is addressed to an imaginary listener so as to rebut in advance all possible objections the listener might have to the underground man's arguments. The distinctive feature of Olesha's own particular narrative dialogicality is the extent to which the addressee is openly identified as another self of the narrator, usually the narrator as child. This marked circularity and self-centeredness of Olesha's fictional dialogue often gives the appearance of a special kind of soliloquy.[1] And indeed, as Bakhtin has observed, the soliloquy is distinguished by a highly dialogical relationship to oneself.[2] It is just this dialogical relationship of Olesha's narrative personae to each other that forms one of the most significant threads connecting his work from different periods.

Other elements of Olesha's work also operate dialogically, including especially its thematics. As is clear in *Envy*, his technique is to set in motion a lively debate among various competing ideas and themes, to state the issues "as an equation of *pro* and *contra*."[3] The fact that he does not declare the winners of the debate has been viewed by critics with various political and ideological axes to grind as a kind of irresponsibility or oversight. The fact is, however, that his dialogical treatment of theme is a consistent feature of his work and one of the primary bases of his special poetics.

Double-voiced Narration and the Search for Childhood

In *No Day without a Line* Olesha wants to restore his life "to the point of distraction" (363) and to be able to experience it again not just intellectually but tactilely. In order to do so he engages in acts of literary conjury. As a boy Olesha liked to cut out play armor from cardboard: "I remembered to the point of hallucination one of the moments when I was engaged in that game. . . . I am holding the cardboard as it turns blue in the twilight. My God, I'll stretch out my hand, and the cardboard will turn up in my hand—and the moment will repeat itself!" (363).

This intense desire to recapture his childhood and the ways in which he saw the world as a child is certainly one of the most powerful impulses, if not the most powerful, behind Olesha's best work. The desire to perceive things as a child no doubt accounts in large measure for Olesha's great affinity for and wide-ranging exploitation of the Shklovskian technique of estrangement. For making the familiar world strange or unfamiliar relies again on the device of showing it as though seen for the first time,[4] a vantage point that is accessible, it may be assumed, only to a child. Olesha's search for childhood is also graphically embodied in and exemplified by his narrative techniques.

Considering that Olesha claims that he is not interested in writing novels in the style of Tolstoy (426), it is perhaps ironic that his own narrative techniques so closely resemble the scheme Tolstoy employs in his novel *Childhood (Detstvo)*. In *Childhood*, as Boris Sorokin has observed, Tolstoy produces a kind of "double vision" by using the point of view of both the child and the adult narrator in tandem with each other.[5] Exactly this point of view constitutes the basic narrative stance in most of Olesha's fiction. If one were to make a composite image of the narrators in Olesha's stories from the late 1920s, it would be that of an adult looking backwards in time, sometimes through the eyes of a child and sometimes through his mature eyes. In some instances Olesha's child narrator is looking forward to future adulthood. In others the reader is not sure exactly which point of view is in control, so that there emerges a blended point of view of the adult and the child. In some works the child's point of view is explicit in the overall narrative structure, but in others infantile or childlike perspectives appear only occasionally in order to present the world as though seen for the first time. Thus the reader often perceives events through a kind of double filter in which there may be constant tension and competition between the child's and the adult's points of view.

The competition that is embedded in Olesha's typical narrative structure is one of the main sources of the tremendously dialogical character of his best works. The voice of the child alternates with and vies with the voice of the adult so that the reader receives a story as though told by means of a double-voiced dialogue.

The narrative structure of *Envy* would appear at first glance to form an exception to the dominant trend in Olesha's narrative techniques. The first part of the novel is told from the point of Kavalerov in the first person. Part two is told in the third person, largely from the implied vantage point of Ivan Babichev. The basic stylistic congruity between the two parts makes for a smooth transition between them.[6] Another aspect of *Envy*'s narrative structure that should be mentioned is the covert presence in the narrative point of view of a child. When Kavalerov describes the way in which Andrei Babichev has taken him in off the streets this child comes out of hiding: "In my life there have even appeared the ivory buttons of a blanket cover, and in them—you just have to find the right spot—there swam the iridescent ring of the spectrum. I recognized them immediately. They had returned to me from the farthest, long forgotten corner of a child's memory" (37).

Here the boy of Kavalerov's childhood steps forward momentarily to reveal one of the mainsprings of Olesha's technique in the novel, and indeed in all of his work: that the many observations in *Envy* about such things as salt falling off the edge of a knife or the visual impressions made by the buttons on a blanket cover are really the kinds of observations a child might make about the world around him. At the same time the reader senses that this child's poetic perception is rather precocious, perhaps too precocious for a child. And in fact the observations made by the narrative persona of *Envy* are often the sort that an adult in search of childhood perspective would make.

The dialogue between the child and the adult appears in various formulations throughout most of Olesha's fiction. In certain stories, such as "The Cherry Stone" and "Love," and in a sketch like "In the World," the basic point of view, as in *Envy*, is that of an adult; but there are also either implicit or explicit manifestations of infantile or childlike points of view whose object is to present the world as though seen for the first time. In other stories the child's point of view asserts itself quite explicitly. If one compares the two autobiographical sketches "I Look into the Past" and "Human Material," the impression arises that Olesha uses them as a kind of narrative workshop. The first words of "I Look into the Past" are "When Bleriot flew across Lamanche I was a little school boy" (220). Here the reader finds the point of view of an adult looking back to his childhood. At the beginning of "Human Material" Olesha reverses this perspective so that the child's point of view is primary, and the child is looking forward into the future: "I am a little school boy. When I grow up I will be just like Mr. Kovalevsky. My whole family demands that of me. I will be an engineer and a homeowner" (226).

Just as there is always a child lurking in Kavalerov's outlook, there is an adult waiting to announce himself in the autobiographical narrator of "Human Material." He eventually does so openly with the words "Now I look around and I don't see any beards! There is no one with a beard!" (227). The narrator of this argumentative autobiography rejoices that now no one is forcing him to be an engineer and that now he can be concerned with justice for the oppressed rather than with the accumulation of wealth for himself. Finally, the narrator says that he is going to strangle that part of himself that wants "to extend his hands to the past" and that he is going to "smother in myself the second 'I,' and the third 'I,' and all the 'I's' who are crawling out from the past" (229). Here Olesha is also carrying on a dialogue with those critics who accused him of dwelling too much on the past. His candor is both disarming and unsettling, because he exposes the method behind his narrative for the purpose of renouncing that which is most dear to him, that is, his several "I's" who constantly make him revisit his childhood.

The kind of narrative technique found in "Human Material" is executed with greater subtlety and to greater effect in "The Chain." This story and "Liompa" stand out as Olesha's greatest achievements in the genre of the short story. In fact, they must be considered high-ranking in the entire corpus of Soviet Russian short stories. In addition to its richly woven stylistic fabric, "The Chain" exhibits Olesha's characteristic narrative structure in its most sophisticated form. The story is told from the first person by a child. The child's point of view is, however, not the only one, not even the controlling one. For behind it, and in competition with it, is the viewpoint of an adult who is looking back on his impressions of youth.

Competition between an adult's point of view and a child's is suggested already at the beginning of "The Chain," where the child narrator is struggling to enter the world of adults and to have his outlook on the world accepted by them. He feels that "I do not have the right to participate in the life of the world. I even feel guilty expressing myself so intelligently: Bleriot . . . The English Channel" (203). The narrator believes that he is better informed than the student, Orlov, who comes to visit his sister, but he feels awkward about declaring this openly.

The narrative of "The Chain" is characterized by subtle shifts between the child's and the adult's points of view. As the narrator sets out on his bicycle ride, his childish point of view is clearly dominant: "Why does an insect, having landed in my eye, immediately perish? Do I really put out poisonous juices?" (204). But as the ride continues, the voice of the adult narrator intrudes and takes over briefly: "The running of the bicycle is accompanied by a sound similar to frying. Sometimes it's as though a firecracker explodes. But that's not important. These are details which you can pile up as many of as you like. You could talk about the cows that have been torn apart from the inside by a skeleton and look like tents. Or about the cows in white suede masks. What's important is that I lost the drive chain. Without it you can't ride a bicycle. The drive chain flew off at full speed, and I noticed it too late" (204–5).

With the words "these are details which you can pile up as many of as you like," the illusion of the child's speech is broken off, and the adult narrator imposes his own point of view. The self-conscious child has momentarily become a self-conscious adult who is drawing attention to the brilliant artifice of his narrative. Soon, however, the point of view of the child narrator reasserts itself: "I am walking and pushing the machine by its fiber handlebar. The pedal hits me below the knee. *Three boys, three boys I don't know are running along the edge of the ravine. They are running away, gilded by the sun.* A blissful weakness arises below my stomach. I understand: the boys have found the chain. They are running in the depth of the landscape" (205; italics added).

In this passage and in others like it in "The Chain" we encounter Olesha's narrative technique at its most subtle and most refined. Chudakova maintains that the description of the three boys, shown here in italics, is "more an illustration to an unknown story than a legitimate part of the story we are reading." Furthermore, this description amounts to "a destruction of the usual literary connections between the hero and what he sees around himself, of the proportions between the 'psychological' part and 'the description'."[7] According to Chudakova, in the realistic tradition what the characters see tells us about their psychological state. In the work of Olesha and some of his contemporaries, however, we are freed of the necessity of such a link. The characters' impressions are not motivated in the conventional way so that "the hero sees that which it seems he ought not to see in his present spiritual condition."[8] In the example at hand, the child narrator's impression of the three boys as "gilded by the sun" is something he ought not be able to see. Having denied that there is a connection between the description and the character's psychological experience, Chudakova hedges somewhat on her thesis by asserting that the boys "gilded by the sun" are the "strange, almost indifferent point of view of a person gripped by fear and desperation."[9] What then is really going on, and what is the significance of Olesha's narrative technique in this passage?

The crucial distinctive feature of the narrative in "The Chain" is its double point of view in which the perceptions of the child are intermingled with those of the adult. As has been shown here, the shifts between these two points of view may take place suddenly and without notice or apparent motivation. The caprice inherent in this particular narrative scheme is both one of its privileges and one of its merits. In some stories Olesha uses the point of view of a child to produce the impression of things seen for the first time. In "The Chain," on the other hand, the adult narrator invades the child's narration in order to provide his own perspective. Thus the two points of view are interwoven with each other and operate almost simultaneously. If we need to establish the origin of the image of the gilded boys, then it seems most likely that this is a product of the adult narrator's imagination rather than that of a child.

At the end of "The Chain" the adult narrator, who has
previously entered the narrative only surreptitiously, introduces
himself overtly.

This is a story about the distant past.
My dream was to have a bicycle. Well then, now I have become a grown-up. And then, the grown-up, I say to myself, the
school boy:
Well, go ahead and ask now. Now I can take revenge for
myself. Speak your cherished wishes. (207)

Here the interplay and dialogue between the child and the
adult that is implicitly embedded in the story's narrative
receives its explicit disclosure. The adult narrator is struck by
the tremendous distance he feels between himself and his
childhood. There was something heroic about his childhood:
"You were a contemporary of the century. Remember? Bleriot
flew across the English Channel" (207). But now he is chubby,
and he has lagged behind: "Now I have stayed behind, look how
I've stayed behind, I am shuffling—a fatman on short legs— . . .
Look, how hard it is for me to run, but I'm running, even though
I'm out of breath, even though my legs get stuck—I'm running
after the thundering storm of the century!"(207). This second
ending of "The Chain," a kind of epilogue, contains one of
Olesha's most famous winged phrases in the image of the fat
man "running after the thundering storm of the century." These
last words of the epilogue dovetail perfectly with the last words
of the story proper.

After losing his chain and engaging in a reverie about what
will happen to him when he gets home, the narrator meets up
with Utochkin, the famous racer of bicycles, cars, and motorcycles. For me reason Utochkin is considered in Odessa to be an
eccentric, the town mad man (gorodskoi sumashedshii) (206).
When Utochkin takes the narrator and his bicycle home in his
car, the narrator suddenly feels a surge of masculinity and bold-
ness that replaces his fear of punishment for having lost the
bicycle chain: "I'm rushing to punish mama, papa, Vera, and the
student. . . . We're men. There he is, a great man: Utochkin!"
(206-7). When they arrive, Utochkin goes up to the student, to
whom the bicycle belongs in the first place, and tells him, "You

shouldn't offend the child. Why have you offended the child? Be so kind as to give him back the chain" (207). As Utochkin drives away from the dacha, the student shouts after the storm that is flying away, "Swine! Charlatan! Mad man!" (207). The description of the "storm that is flying away" paves the way for the last words of the story about the "thundering storm of the century" and thereby gives the double conclusions to the story an effective stylistic symmetry.

The surprise denouement with its humorous twist in which Utochkin accuses the student of taking the chain to his own bicycle gives the ending of the story a delicious ambiguity. Did the narrator, who fantasizes taking revenge on the student, make up a story for Utochkin that the student had taken the chain to his, the narrator's, bicycle? Or was the narrator's story so garbled by his fear of punishment and his awe of Utochkin that the facts became confused? Or did Utochkin, who is both impetuous and rash, simply interpret the narrator's story in a way that suited his own fancy? Certainly one or another permutation of these possibilities took place, but Olesha leaves it to the reader to decide. Thus Olesha achieves yet another double effect at the end: he brings the action to a neat conclusion but leaves the significance of the events ambiguous. "The Chain" is an excellent example of Olesha's ability to create a tightly knit plot with its weight on the ending.

In "The Chain" Olesha does more than simply point to the great events of the day or note the existence of the enigmatic Utochkin. He integrates the heroic motif of the channel crossing into the story's fabric not just as a fact to behold in wonder but as an effective means of revealing the character of the young narrator. Olesha also incorporates the character of Utochkin, one of his real childhood heroes, into the story with a superb blend of sympathy, awe, wry humor, and irony. The linchpin of this story's effectiveness, though, is the double-voiced dialogue that takes place between the two sides of the narrative persona. In this dialogue youth's perceptions of adulthood and age's perceptions of youth reflect mutually on each other, producing the story's elusive ambiguity and great poignancy. Together with the expertly crafted plot, the pithy exposition of character, and gemlike style, this dialogue makes "The Chain" one of Olesha's true masterpieces.

A Dialogue between Life and Death

If "The Chain" has an equal among Olesha's short stories, it is the story "Liompa." While both Olesha and most of his critics consider *Envy* to be his greatest achievement, it is possible that "Liompa" is the author's most artistically perfect work[10]—for "Liompa" is one of those fortuitous instances when an author exploits all of his strengths to their utmost while simultaneously realizing the fullest potential of the genre he is working in.

Although the quality of "Liompa" is evident, the overall significance of the story is far more elusive and controversial because the story is genuinely difficult to read, and a first reading is unlikely to produce any firm conclusions.[11] In this instance Olesha does not make the reading of the text difficult in the self-conscious Shklovskian manner found in other places, where devices are frequently shown off for the reader to note. In "Liompa" the story's difficulty inheres rather in its intricately woven network of references and motifs. There are other ways in which "Liompa" appears at first glance to differ radically from most of Olesha's other stories. Rather than an intensely personal, almost confessional narrative point of view, there is a largely objective third-person stance of omniscience. Instead of a festive or holiday atmosphere, there is an acute analysis of the psychological process of a person's dying. There is also no mention of the burning social issues that often preoccupy Olesha's characters.

Closer examination reveals that "Liompa" is comprised of many elements and motifs that are typical of Olesha. In this story they appear in an untypical arrangement, however, one of the features of "Liompa" that makes it so distinctive. For example, even though the narrative point of view is of a largely neutral third person, this narrator shows the reader the world from a perspective that alternates between that of an adult and that of a child. Thus, the complex, dual narrative points of view of a child and an adult that are explicit in a story such as "The Chain" are only implicit in "Liompa."

The story is set in springtime: "It was spring, the doors were left open, grass grew by the step, and water that had been spilled on a stone sparkled" (191). One expects a story by Olesha to be set in either spring or summer, but the contrast with the theme of death seems paradoxical. Andrew Barratt has even suggested that "the choice of the springtime setting for a story about death offends against one of the most pervasive literary traditions."[12] The meaning of the spring setting, which is masterfully understated and muted in this story by comparison with many other places in Olesha's work where it is openly celebrated, emerges fully only at the story's conclusion.

The cast of characters in "Liompa" is also familiar. Ponomarev, the dying man, is obviously a representative of the older generation. In "Liompa," unlike many of the stories and *Envy*, the man of the older generation does not serve any socially or politically representative function. Ponomarev's death is shown taking place on a purely personal level. The generational conflict that is found in *Envy* and so many of Olesha's other works is here stripped of its social and ideological aspects and is thereby raised to a higher intellectual and philosophical plane.[13] There are two representatives of the younger generation, the boy Alexander, and the young child who is called in the story "the rubber boy" (*rezinovyi mal'chik*). Alexander is actually in a kind of intermediate stage, since he "acts completely as an adult" (192) in most respects, much like the child narrator in "The Chain" who believes that he is intellectually on a par with adults. The rubber boy is, however, a true child. He provides the strongest foil to the dying Ponomarev, who openly envies him.

The three characters are largely defined in relation to each other by their relationship to the things around them. Ponomarev's situation is made unbearable by the fact that things are disappearing from him: "Countries disappeared, America, the chance to be handsome or rich, a family" (192). All that these things have left Ponomarev are their names. But the names are also slipping away, and thus he struggles at the end of the story to give a name to the rat he hears in the kitchen. Alexander, on the other hand, is a complete master of the things that surround him, a characteristic highlighted by the fact that he is building a model airplane correctly and according to the diagram and that he "knows the laws"(192). The rubber boy is only just coming into consciousness of the world around him: "Every second created a new thing for him" (193), but he does not understand the significance of these things.

Barratt has made an extensive and penetrating analysis of "Liompa," one which is well worth examining in some detail. According to Barratt, the differences among Ponomarev, Alexander, and the rubber boy are only differences of degree, since they each represent a stage of life through which each man passes. In "Liompa" Ponomarev has a revelation that his belief that he controlled things was mistaken. As Barratt points out, Ponomarev comes to understand that his solipsism was "ridiculously extreme":[14] "I thought that my eye and ear governed things, I thought that the world would cease to exist when I ceased to exist. . . . But I still exist! Why do things not exist? . . . They have gone from me, and only their names . . . swirl in my brain. But what am I to do with these names?" (193).

In the passage immediately preceding this one, Olesha describes Isaac Newton sitting in an orchard: "Tiny ants ran among the mounds. Newton sat in the orchard. In the apple there was hidden a multitude of causes able to call forth an even greater multitude of effects" (193). Barratt believes Olesha is suggesting here that Newton, who sees the apple only as an illustration of the law of gravity, does not realize that it is also part of "the chain of life." Barratt concludes that Liompa is an "extreme and unambiguous statement of Olesha's critique of pure reason and of the conventional modes of thinking which derive from the modern scientific tradition extending back to Newton."[15]

According to Barratt, Olesha battles against the Newtonian modern scientific tradition because it stifles man's inventiveness and imagination. Olesha is fond of spectacle because it has the power to "destroy or suspend the influence of scientific knowledge on our manner of perception." In "Liompa," however, the possibility of suspending the laws imposed on us by scientific knowledge is denied to Ponomarev. In the final analysis, therefore, "In 'Liompa' he [Olesha] reveals the precariousness, and the ultimate absurdity of man's imagined grasp of his physical environment, and raises it to the level of tragedy."[16]

There is certainly much to recommend Barratt's interpretation of "Liompa." As has been seen here, Olesha's use of the spectacular to destroy or at least to suspend the laws of physics is one of the dominant principles of his work, and he constantly shows how tenuous is man's control of the physical world. Yet, even if man's solipsism is ridiculous or absurd, Olesha does not intend to renounce it because it is just this solipsism in the other stories of the *Cherry Stone* cycle that helps man to break through or suspend physical laws and create an alternate world for himself. This alternate world may prove to be illusory and burdensome, but it is usually beneficial, sometimes even necessary, rarely if ever harmful. It is indisputable that in "Liompa" Ponomarev does not have the chance to engage in this liberating form of solipsism. In this respect, Ponomarev's fate does indeed appear to be tragic. The conclusion of "Liompa," however, is far more problematic than Barratt allows, because it involves a great deal more than simply the resolution of Ponomarev's fate.

The structure of "Liompa" is profoundly dialogical in the Bakhtinian sense that its constituent elements are contrapuntally juxtaposed to one another.[17] As such it is strongly resistant to the imposition of finalizing or monological interpretations on it. In "Liompa" Olesha does not simply make a static juxtaposition of Ponomarev with "the rubber boy" but rather shows them in a dynamic state of tension, even competition. This tension is underscored when the rubber boy comes to look at Ponomarev on his deathbed and out of spite Ponomarev tries to frighten him by saying, "You know, when I die, nothing will remain. Not the yard, not the tree, not papa, not mama. I'll take everything with me" (193). In addition, the story's underlying central opposition between life and death takes the form of Ponomarev's struggle to hang on to the things of his experience and their names. And, the kitchen, which is bursting with the life of the tenants and the rat, is juxtaposed with the dying world of Ponomarev's bedroom.[18] There is also competition between animate objects, inanimate objects, and even abstractions in the mind of Ponomarev. He is worried not just about the loss of things but also about the loss of the chance to be rich and handsome, as well as the chance to have a family.

Ponomarev's struggle to give the rat a name is particularly interesting. It is on one level his last attempt to regain some mastery over the world that is inexorably receding from his power to control it. By naming the rat he will be placing an abstraction, a name, on a living being, and thereby gaining not just control, however illusory, but understanding of it. The name Ponomarev finally blurts out, "Liompa," is not only un-Russian in its sound, but it also suggests more the name of an inanimate thing than an animate being. The merging or, better, the interchangeablity of inanimate characteristics with animate ones is reflected not just in the name of the rat but in the description of the "rubber boy," who has the attributes of an inanimate substance. In "Liompa" Olesha is not just analyzing the way in which man relates to and apprehends the objects around him. He is also demonstrating the mutable, dynamic, unstable nature of those objects and their relationships to each other: "A bicycle leaned against the wall by its pedal. The pedal had made a scratch in the wallpaper. It was as though the bicycle supported itself by this scratch on the wall" (183). The nature of things and their relationships to each other depend on the perspective from which they are viewed. When the little boy visits Ponomarev he sees an optical illusion, but as soon as he starts toward it the "change in distance destroyed the illusion" (193).

The end of "Liompa" contains another important example of the mutability of things depending on the perspective from which they are viewed, as well as other keys to the story's overall meaning. When Ponomarev dies a coffin is brought in:

> In the afternoon a sky-blue coffin with yellow decorations appeared in the kitchen. The rubber boy looked from the corridor, crossing his hands behind his back. They had to turn the coffin every which way for a long time in order to carry it in the door. They bumped into a shelf, a saucepan, and some plaster fell down. The boy Alexander climbed up on the stove and helped, supporting the box from below. When the coffin finally penetrated into the corridor, it immediately became black, and the rubber boy, shuffling his sandals, ran ahead.
>
> "Grandpa! Grandpa!" he cried. "They've brought you a coffin." (194)

This conclusion is remarkable for the succinct yet subtle way in which it both recapitulates the major themes and motifs of the story and suggests their ultimate significance. What this passage demonstrates is that even after Ponomarev's death, man's struggle to master the things around him continues. The wrestling with the coffin and the crashing into objects in the kitchen are graphic illustrations of this struggle. The boy Alexander's climbing up onto the stove in order to help hold the coffin shows that man will continue to battle against Newton's law of gravity. The difficulty in dealing with the coffin also hints that things will continue to be unmanageable, perhaps even inscrutable. By locating the activity surrounding the coffin in the kitchen Olesha reiterates the kitchen's status as the locus of the story's lively activity. In returning the action of the story to the place where it begins, Olesha not only gives the story a neat structural symmetry but also suggests that even in the face of death, life continues.

Olesha has already developed the notion that life will go on in a number of ways. As Kazimiera Ingdahl has pointed out, the apple Newton sees in the orchard is a symbol of life and death in which "we can discern the circular life cycle."[19] Even the rat is a dualistic symbol of both life and death:[20] the rat's moving around in the kitchen signifies liveliness, but Ponomarev thinks that uttering the rat's name will mean death for him. But the most dramatic suggestion that life continues after death is found at the end of the story in the presence of the two boys who help carry in the coffin of Ponomarev. Throughout the story they are the most important representatives of life's continual force. It is inconceivable that Olesha, who so masterfully crafts every phrase and every epithet in "Liompa," does not intend their participation in the final scene of the story to carry substantial meaning. And in fact, their involvement at the end of the story means that Ponomarev's death and his failure to come to grips with the world around him is not a final or necessarily tragic event. For the boys clearly represent not just the continuation of life but its constant renewal.

So far we have noted the struggle with the coffin, but not the coffin itself. When it lies in the light of the kitchen it is sky-blue (goluboi) with yellow decorations, but in the dark of the corridor it turns black. Again, it is beyond question that Olesha invests this juxtaposition with great significance. The change in coloration is a succinct way of restating the motif of the mutability of things in different environments and different perspectives. But here the switch in color is not simply an illustration of objects' changeability. The colors blue and yellow, especially in a decorative pattern, suggest celebration and gaiety, and black, needless to say, symbolizes death. Thus, the coffin contains simultaneously within itself both the possibility for the celebration of death and death itself. The idea that death may be celebrated is reinforced by the rubber boy's calling out to the dead Ponomarev that they have brought him a coffin. In his eyes the bringing in of the coffin is an event that is festive in a way an adult would not usually perceive it to be. His cry then is not simply a case of unconscious irony or humor.[21]

As has just been noted here, "Liompa" recasts and reinterprets familiar Oleshan elements in unfamiliar and sometimes surprising ways. One of these is a subtle but nevertheless perceptible suggestion of a carnivalistic outlook on life. For in the conclusion to "Liompa," indeed throughout the course of the story, Olesha evokes a principle that is fundamental to the carnival view of the world. As Bakhtin puts it, "Old age is pregnant, death is gestation."[22] In the carnival and in the carnivalistic approach to life, death is celebrated, partly because it contains within itself both renewal and rebirth.

In the context of "Liompa," the very pairing of the old, dying Ponomarev with the young, active boys has powerful carnivalistic overtones. The juxtaposition of youth and age and the succession of old and new are constant themes of the carnival that have their origins in the carnival's basic duality of life and death. That "Liompa" should be set in the springtime is not simply a paradox or a reflexive action on the part of Olesha. Spring is the time of year when the carnival that celebrates the renewal of life after winter takes place. Even the contemporary Mardi Gras celebrations, while certainly a weak echo of the genuine, medieval carnival, preserve this particular element. Spring is also the time of year when young boys make model airplanes and run after them. At the very moment that he dies, the last thing Ponomarev sees is Alexander chasing after his airplane. This moment contains in a brilliantly capsulized form the epitome of the simultaneity and the interrelatedness of life and death found both in the carnival and in "Liompa." In the dialogue Olesha creates in "Liompa" the spring setting and the lively activities of the young boys act as a counterweight to Ponomarev's death and his failure to maintain his grasp on things. They are the light, gay side of life that is in competition with the dark, troubled side of life symbolized by Ponomarev. The interaction and struggle of light and dark, life and death that are the fulcrum of "Liompa" suggest not so much finality or tragedy as the continuity and duality of the carnival.

A Return to Dialogue and Belated Footnotes

No Day without a Line is remarkable for the ways in which it recapitulates many of the salient features of Olesha's earlier prose and makes postscripts to its central themes and motifs. In a sense he takes up in No Day without a Line where he left off in his best fiction of the late 1920s. One of the most conspicuous manifestations of this is his return to his most compelling theme, his own youth. During the 1930s Olesha had attempted in a work like *A Strict Youth* to make the treatment of the new Soviet youth into a surrogate for his real interest. In *No Day without a Line* he comes back to his main enduring genuine concern: himself. As in his early stories one of his principal mechanisms for dealing with this subject is the creation of a dialogue between age and youth and life and death. The dialogues of *No Day without a Line* often take the form of imaginative representations of discourses with Olesha's several selves: Olesha the child, Olesha the poet, and Olesha the athlete. In one place Olesha, who had a stepson but no children of his own,[23] even imagines himself as a father.

In *No Day without a Line* Olesha's narrative persona is constantly trying to move in two directions at the same time: trying to recapture his youth and saying goodbye to the world. Restoring life and parting with life are in *No Day without a Line* part of the same process of setting one's accounts straight and coming to some sort of understanding about the meaning of life and death in one's old age. Even the effort at returning to one's childhood is bittersweet, because the pleasure of reconstructing youth is mixed with regret that youth is lost forever. In Odessa the road to Lanzheron holds a number of poignant memories for Olesha. He prefaces one of them with the exclamation "Farewell, road to Lanzheron, farewell!" (371). There follows a description of how the narrator watched his father and his cousin, Tolya, play billiards and drink beer: "It was terribly pleasant for me to watch how they drank beer. I myself didn't want to drink at all, on the contrary, beer always spoke to me of castor oil, but seeing how they drowned their mustaches, which then shook under the weight of the foam, I envied them—I wanted quickly to become a grownup" (371).

In this passage the acts of re-creating life and saying goodbye to it are merged explicitly. The persona of the young boy through whose eyes we witness the beer drinking is looking forward to his adulthood, while the adult uses him to recall an experience from his youth. Here is the epitome of the forwards and backwards, backwards and forwards perspectives of *No Day without a Line.* Here too is illustrated in capsule form the underlying narrative structure of the book, which has at its basis the dialogically juxtaposed viewpoints of an old man and a young boy. In several passages the dialogue between these two competing points of view is revealed with great clarity. One of Olesha's favorite similes is his characterization of falling leaves as creaking ships. He wonders, "Then I didn't think that they [the leaves] creaked like ships, that comes into mind now. But, however, perhaps I thought about it then too!" (264–65). This dialogue between the adult and the boy is continued in connection with the author's recollections of his grandmother escorting him to take the entrance examinations for the gymnasium:

> My grandmother brought a writer, and also a little boy. He did not see everything that the writer recalls now. Perhaps all of that never was! No, it was after all! Undoubtedly, it was autumn and the leaves were falling. . . . Undoubtedly, sailing past me their sides creaked like ships. And, like ships, sailing around me, they described a circle. . . . No, the boy saw all of that—the writer only recalls it now and draws it from other recollections, but it was that very boy whose grandmother brought him who saw.
>
> And indeed, where is the borderline? Where did he begin to see? Where was he simply a boy and then suddenly became a poet? And on that morning—oh, undoubtedly—he both looked and saw. (378–79)

Although Olesha is probably not consciously aware of it, in this part of *No Day without a Line* he provides the reader with a disclosure of the genesis of his basic narrative strategy in such early stories as "The Chain" and "I Look into the Past." By trying to establish which part of him, the young boy or the adult writer, is responsible for his artistic perceptions of the world, he reveals the source of competition inherent in his dual narrative structure, where the voice of the child competes with the voice of the grownup. It is this highly dialogical structure of many parts of *No Day without a Line* that brings it back into contact with Olesha's best early short fiction.

One of the recurrent leitmotifs of *No Day without a Line* is leave taking. Near the end of the book Olesha writes, "I will have to write a book about parting with the world" (558). An earlier passage gives a rather enigmatic variation on this motif: "I will part with you solemnly once again, choosing a special situation, but for now this is a parting in reminiscence" (446). There follows a description of how he once ate a chicken on the way back to the apartment he shared with Ilia I'lf. Olesha concludes this note with the words "There is one of my rough draft partings, dear life" (446). The meaning of this particular reminiscence is not clear, although we know that he considers the period in which he worked for *The Whistle* and lived with Il'f, the same period in which he wrote much of his major work, to be a special one. It is possible that the account of how he bought a whole chicken but did not eat all of it because he felt that it was more than one person ought to consume is meant to suggest that the author did not understand how fortunate he was in this earlier time and was consequently wasteful of his talents. Without a more fully developed context, however, this passage remains, as Olesha says, a rough draft.

Olesha's theme of saying goodbye to the things of the world has its best literary expression in the story "Liompa," where Ponomarev frantically tries to part with the objects around him before he dies. As noted, "Liompa" is something of an enigma among his early works in the sense that, although it treats this theme with tremendous power, it is virtually the only story by Olesha that does. Unlike many of his other stories, which have one or even several companion pieces on similar subjects, "Liompa" seems to stand alone. It is not until the emergence of *No Day without a Line* that Olesha provides a complement and something of a belated footnote to "Liompa."[24]

In *No Day without a Line* the narrator writes that he is afraid he is losing contact with the world around him. In the springtime he wonders why he does not catch the familiar smell of the first signs of spring: "Perhaps, with the years the possibility of this contact is lost?" (556). He wonders whether he can reestablish contact by going out of the city into the country: "Once I wanted to eat nature, brush my cheek against the trunk of a tree, scraping the skin till it bled. Once, arriving in the country for the first time after an absence, I ran up a little hill, and not seeing that there was a cemetery nearby, feeling ecstatic, fell face down into the feet of the grass, which wounded me, and I cried from the feeling of closeness to the earth, and conversed with the earth" (556).

When the narrator arises from the ground, however, his eye catches sight of the cemetery. In symbolic terms this short sketch represents the obverse of the story "Liompa." Whereas in "Liompa" life is affirmed in death, in this sketch death makes its presence felt even as the narrator communes ecstatically with the life-giving power of nature. Thus, both the sketch and "Liompa" depict the dichotomy of life and death as a dialogue in which each side always asserts its rights and never gives in to the hegemony of the other. While Olesha's sketch in *No Day without a Line* lacks the great artistic power of "Liompa," it is nevertheless testimony to the fact that in *No Day without a Line* he has indeed succeeded in resurrecting his skill as a writer to a high level.

In *No Day without a Line* Olesha is greatly preoccupied with death and aging. As with the book's other major themes, he gives these a thoroughly metaliterary treatment, which includes reminiscences, terse statements of belief, passages of literary criticism, short independent sketches, and individual metaphors. The reminiscences of *No Day without a Line* include a number of sections that comprise a kind of necrology of Olesha's contemporaries in which the author bids them farewell. He also examines the processes of aging and of dying but is greatly more interested in the former than in the latter. Olesha dismisses Tolstoy's depiction of Ivan Ilich's death as "healthy nonsense"; he is convinced that when Tolstoy himself died he did not understand a thing and that his death had nothing in common with the death of Ivan Ilich (552). The phenomenon of aging, however, may be described thus: "One of the sensations of aging is that sensation when you don't feel in yourself the shoots of the future. They could always be felt, now another would grow up, begin to give color and smell. Now they are completely gone. The future has disappeared in me!" (551). In this passage the sense of loss experienced in the act of aging is compensated for by the author's transparent glee at inventing an expressive extended metaphor with which to describe that process.

Olesha's Several Selves

When Olesha was working together with the producers of his cartoon comedy, *A Little Girl at the Circus* (*Devochka v tsirke*) (1958), and they asked him what was going to come next, he always replied that he did not know and that it was not he who was writing the cartoon but some other person inside of him.[25] In several passages of *No Day without a Line* Olesha's ability to detach one aspect of himself from another takes the graphic form of dialogues between himself and his several other selves. One of the most intriguing of these involves the manifestation of something like an entirely separate alter ego. Once when visiting a bakery he usually shops at, Olesha's narrator undergoes "a surprising experience, which sometimes visits me and which I call 'the world without me' " (544). The narrator promises to recount this experience in greater detail later, but there is no explicit follow-up to this passage in *No Day without a Line*. Nevertheless, there is a short sketch in which the narrator describes in detail a relationship with a daughter he never had:

> Sometimes through the real circumstances of my life, through its situation, through the things and walls of my home, show through images of some other life, also mine, but taking place not always perceptibly for me, not always, so to speak, in my view. . . . I never had children. Suddenly for an instant I feel that these are the children of my daughter. I never had a daughter.
>
> Yes, but I have come to see my daughter. I am her father and grandfather. I am visiting my daughter and grandchildren when they have been waiting for me to come to dinner. . . . I have brought a cake. My god, how I remember the square of cake that was awkward to carry! (458)

Olesha's description here of "images of another life" confirms what Paustovsky characterized as his ability to create with his imagination a special life for himself out of the reality that surrounded him.[26] In *No Day without a Line* the narrator is constantly aware of other selves living within himself, expressed most often by the dialogue between an older self and a younger self. Sometimes Olesha depicts this dialogue in the form of a miniature sketch. One sketch begins with the passage quoted above in which the narrator announces that the plot of his book is about how a man lived to old age:

> Since nothing happens to the sensation that "I live" and it remains the same as it was in infancy, with this sensation I perceive myself, an old man, youthfully, freshly, and that old man is unusually new for me. . . . And suddenly in the mirror at the young me, who is within and without, looks an old man.
>
> Fantastic! Theater! When going away from the mirror, I lie

down on a couch and I don't think about myself that I am the
one who I have just seen. No, I am lying in the capacity of the
same "I" who was lying when I was a boy. And the other one
has remained in the mirror. Now there are two of us, I and
he. . . .

"Hello, who are you?"

"I am you."

"It's not true."

Sometimes I even laugh. And the one in the mirror laughs.
I laugh until I cry. And the one in the mirror cries. (459)

In Olesha's works the mirror is often connected with the appearance of a character's double. In the beginning of the second
part of *Envy* Kavalerov's looking into a mirror presages the appearance of Ivan Babichev, his partner in conspiracy and
carnivalistic double. In his speech to the First Congress of the
Soviet Writers' Union, Olesha talks about the ability that people,
especially artists, have for feeling a double within themselves.[27] In
addition to being able to sense a double within himself, Olesha
has a great capacity for creating double characters in his fiction, as
Envy and his stories demonstrate. In *No Day without a Line,*
where Olesha deliberately reduces his means of expression to
their barest essentials, there are for all practical purposes no other
characters than the author-narrator. Yet, the multiple personalities of the narrative persona embrace nearly all of the characters
that are essential to Olesha: the child, the adult, the writer-poet,
and the athlete. He describes the last of these: "For me there is no
doubt that in me still lives someone powerful, some
athlete—more accurately, the wreckage of an athlete, a torso
without arms and legs, turning around heavily in my body and
thereby tormenting both me and himself" (457).

Here the presence of a double within the narrator's persona is
not an object of fascination and wonder, not a person to chat with,
laugh with, and cry with. In this case the visitation of one's
double brings discomfort to both the young man and the old one.
Olesha expresses the sense of loss of one's youthful physical
capacities by means of an image he associates with himself all
throughout his lifetime, the image of the strong, young athlete.
All of his life, and decades after he had given up active participation in any sort of physical activity, Olesha continued to view part
of himself as a trackman or a soccer player. He continued to

regard himself, as did his contemporary and follower, Sergei Bondarin, as an "overweight forward."[28]

In *No Day without a Line* Olesha's act of reconstructing his
youth is also intended to play a trick on the forces of nature, that
is, to trick them into believing as he does that in the final analysis
he is really immortal. Throughout the book Olesha's narrator
vacillates between hoping for the trick to work and the realization
that it cannot. The conclusion to one of his miniatures in which
his younger self yields to his older self makes a concession that
the triumph of death is inevitable. When he was a boy and people
cried out "boy" to someone else, he would turn around also:

> Will I turn around now when they cry, "Old man!"
> Perhaps I won't turn around. Don't want to? No, I think
> that basically the surprise is that it has come so quickly. . . .
> Has it really come?
> "Old man! Hey, Old man!"
> No, it's not me, it can't be.
> "Old man!"
> No, I won't turn around. It can't be that it has happened so
> quickly.
> "Old man! There, the fool doesn't turn around! It's
> me—death!" (547)

This passage then appears to be the inescapable end of the dialogue between the narrator's youthful and aged sides, when the
old man has to give up the illusion that by conversing with his
younger double he can somehow remain young himself and
forestall the natural order of things, when he has to confront
death on his own. Yet, Olesha states in another place that
"Nevertheless there is the absolute conviction that I won't die"
(552). As with the other major thematic juxtapositions of *No
Day without a Line*, such as success and failure, restoration and
deterioration, age and youth, Olesha does not give the contest between life and death a definitive denouement. In this fashion he
remains faithful to the dialogical dynamic that is at the heart of
his major artistic accomplishments.

Valentin Kataev believes that in *No Day without a Line*,
"Olesha's discovery is to show the process of the appearance and
construction of an artistic image. It is as though Olesha verbally
reproduces the very course of his artistic thinking."[29] Olesha's

self-conscious Shklovskian technique of showing off the processes by which he creates his images is found not just in this book but in virtually all of his work. The numerous circular dialogues with the different manifestations of Olesha's narrative selves epitomize the high degree to which *No Day without a Line* is self-directed and self-absorbed, almost an extended soliloquy. One may even wonder whether the reader has been invited to take part in this self-centered dialogue at all. In fact, as Kataev obliquely suggests, Olesha constantly summons the reader to participate as a witness to his creative processes. When he complains that he has an illness of the sentence, he is in effect telling the reader to watch him at work and see how clever he still is, despite the appearance that he is old and decrepit. It is undeniable that to a certain extent Olesha is exploiting a kind of calculated self-pity in order to gain the reader's sympathies. Yet, he elicits from the reader more than just sympathy and the passive role of an eyewitness to his artistic wizardry. The great dialogicality of his work inexorably draws the reader into his dialogical debates, forcing the reader to decide matters. However much they are based on false premises and assumptions about fiction in general and Olesha in particular, the numerous controversies surrounding his work illustrate how actively engaged his readers and critics are.

The Ramifications of Ambivalence

One of the reasons Olesha's work is so dialogical is that he has such a highly developed ability to see both sides, sometimes several sides, of an issue, theme, or character simultaneously. Another product of this feature of Olesha's vision that is closely related to his great dialogicality is his perpetual ambivalence. For the most part, ambivalence in Olesha plays a productive role. There are, however, some instances where Olesha's unwillingness or inability to resolve certain questions may work to the detriment of a given work. Such is the case in his scenario *A Strict Youth*. At the end of *A Strict Youth* Masha does not make a choice between her husband, Stepanov, and Grisha Fokin, so the mainspring of the dramatic interest in the scenario is left unresolved. In the context of Olesha's idealization of Soviet youth and his depiction of good characters, such as Stepanov, versus better characters, such as Fokin, this lack of dramatic resolution does not so much inspire the reader to figure things out as it leaves a nebulous impression of saccharine ambiguity and irresolution.

In another instance Olesha's ambivalence may have led to a kind of artistic paralysis that prevented him from giving a potentially important work a finished form. He begins his article "Remarks of a Dramatist" with the sensational words "I am interested in the question of the physical destruction of characters in plays."[30] He is also interested in the philosophical and moral questions associated with murder and killing, as the several drafts of "The Death of Sand" (*Smert' Zanda*) and *The Black Man* (*Chernyi chelovek*) illustrate. "Sand" was published in an unfinished form in 1930, and part of the play "The Black Man" was published as a fragment in 1932, but neither of these ever resulted in a completed work.[31] In *The Black Man* Sand interviews a man who has committed a crime of passion when he attempted to murder another man out of jealousy. The problem of the conscience of someone who kills is highlighted in this fragment by references to Raskol'nikov's murder of the old pawnbroker in *Crime and Punishment* and to the killing that was done in the name of the Revolution. Elizabeth Beaujour believes that Olesha never finished *Sand/Black Man* because to do so would have meant revealing too much of his own true self.[32] It also seems likely that he never completed these works because his attitude toward killing, especially killing on the stage, never became firmly established. The alternate endings to *A Conspiracy of Feelings* are eloquent testimony to this attitude. As it turns out, Olesha's fullest treatment of his Sand theme may be found in this play, where Ivan Babichev encourages Kavalerov to murder Andrei and casually suggests to someone that he kill the husband of his mistress.

There are of course some places where Olesha casts off his characteristic ambivalence in favor of definite moral conclusions. Generally speaking, however, the artistic quality of these works suffers by comparison with works in which true dialogue is maintained. This is especially evident in some of the sketches where Olesha portrays his battles with the older generation not so much as a dynamic struggle but as a kind of pat hand in which his own views are clearly victorious.

There is also the potential danger that Olesha's talent for seeing both sides of an idea may lead not to dialogue but to excessive schematism. One work where he treads a fine line between such schematism and true dialogue is "The Cherry Stone." The optimistic conclusion of this story, in which the seed planted by Avel will grow into a cherry tree in the courtyard of the concrete colossus, strongly suggests that amicable resolutions between the contesting forces of sensitivity and practicality, romanticism and realism, and imagination and the plan will take place.[33] Yet, Olesha refrains from portraying these resolutions as inevitable and thereby preserves the kind of dialogue between competing ideas that makes his best works so provocative.

Olesha's refusal to take sides has earned the reproach of critics in both the Soviet Union and abroad from the time his works first appeared until now. His play *A List of Blessings*, his strongest dramatic work, is an excellent case in point, and the critical response to it is therefore worth examining in some detail. Not surprisingly, most of the criticism of the play has centered on its questions of social classes and their relationships. One of the most typical responses to *List*, expressed by Yu. Yuzovsky, is that the heroine Goncharova's theme of loneliness is a "petty-bourgeois treatment of the idea of personality and the collective."[34] A. Prozorov seconds this interpretation, and calls Goncharova's acceptance of the proletariat, based as it is on the old feelings of love and pity, nothing more than "the other side of her petty-bourgeois individualism."[35] Some critics took great pains to refute the play's most quoted and memorable line, Goncharova's winged saying that "in an epoch of rapid tempos the artist should think slowly" (P 95). Prozorov interprets this saying as a defense of Goncharova's Hamletism of the personality divided within itself and claims that what Olesha really means by it is a plea that the intelligentsia be allowed to slow down the process of its reconstruction. For Prozorov the play is too abstract and too far removed from the concrete problems of socialist construction. What Prozorov wants is for Olesha to show Goncharova's future and her conquering of her own past.[36]

In fact, rather than any definite social or ideological line, *A List of Blessings* reflects more ideological ambivalence, exactly the kind of ambivalence the heroine Goncharova experiences.[37] For example, Europe, the repository of so much valued tradition, is portrayed in an almost entirely negative way in *A List of Blessings*. Europe's cultural heritage, which Goncharova feels so close to, is only alluded to. Although she says that she feels at home in her European surroundings, Goncharova is never directly shown experiencing her newfound happiness. All of her direct contact with European life that takes place in the play is thoroughly besmirched with corruption and avarice. Of the French characters met in Paris, only the Communist Santillant is shown to be a person of honor and principle. Among the Russian émigrés, most of whom are crooks and cowards, Tregubova stands out as the only one with a semblance of integrity.

Goncharova's fate remains an ambiguous one. While she repents of her doubts about the Soviet system, she appears equally determined to maintain the integrity of her own personal values and convictions in a spirit of greater understanding with the working class. Her demise at the end of the play leaves unresolved the question of whether she will be able, or whether she will be allowed, to realize some sort of synthesis of her two lists in the Soviet Union, one of its blessings and one of its crimes. At the same time, her death has heroic overtones, since she dies in the defense of the revolutionary, Santillant.

Olesha often frustrates his readers and critics when he does not give clear-cut solutions to the questions found in his works. Rudnitsky has expressed this frustration colorfully in his assessment that *A List of Blessings* "began sharply and boldly, but at the end it wagged its tail."[38] Yet, as with *Envy*, the strength of *A List of Blessings* lies not in the solving of problems but in the acuteness with which Olesha poses them. Furthermore, the problematic conclusion of *A List of Blessings* is fully in concert with the heroine Goncharova's character. Another ending might have better satisfied Soviet critics in search of clear moral lessons to be learned, but it probably would have violated the profoundly ambivalent nature of both the play's heroine and its author.

The open-ended nature of the conclusion to *Envy* not only violates readers' expectations about novelistic structure but infuriates critics who are determined to find solutions and clear messages in Olesha. Andrew Barratt considers *Envy* to be a "profoundly disturbing and nihilistic book, particularly for the reader who is intent on discovering a 'message.'" He views *Envy* as a nihilistic work largely because it does not pose a solution to man's existential dilemma.[39] Here it seems that Barratt is stretching a point, since lack of resolution to fundamental conflicts and problems, or even lack of a well-defined philosophy, is not necessarily evidence of a nihilistic view of the world.

The ambivalence inherent in much of Olesha's work has produced apparently unreconcilable differences that have arisen in connection with their critical interpretation. One such case concerns *No Day without a Line*. Chudakova, who usually stresses the lighter aspects of Olesha, believes that it is basically an "unhappy book" because it deals so much with the problems of the author's having forgotten how to write: "In this book there is not the joy which simply bursts from his first books, of which there is a great deal even in *Envy*, where completely different plans battle fiercely and are not resolved. The book was written already not with 'pleasure,' but with bitterness, with desperation."[40]

Skhlovsky, perhaps partly from the desire to refute Chudakova conclusively, finds that "Olesha's last book is optimistic, it flies up above the everyday (*byt*), it casts off childhood in order not to return to it."[41] Here Shklovsky is surely carried away with his own paradoxical poeticism, for in *No Day without a Line*, far from casting off childhood, Olesha constantly uses it in juxtaposition with his adulthood as one of the principal themes of the book. Attempting to recapture childhood has implications both bitter and sweet, just as examining one's old age does. As has been shown here, the essence of *No Day without a Line* is neither optimism nor pessimism, but the manner in which these two conflicting emotions and other antithetical emotions and ideas compete with each other in an intense dialogue that grants none of them a complete victory.

Both Barratt and Chudakova, as well as others, stress the lack of resolution in Olesha of the questions his works place before the reader. Chudakova also notes the way in which the different elements of *Envy* actually seem to combat each other. For decades now critics both in the Soviet Union and the West have been struggling with such matters as who represents what, with whom does the author most closely sympathize, and who is ultimately on the side of right in *Envy*, the stories, *A List of Blessings*, and Olesha's other works. This debate is natural because of the provocative manner in which Olesha depicts a number of fundamental issues concerning the position of the Soviet intelligentsia, especially that of the artist, in the emerging Soviet society. In a sense, however, all of these explorations are doomed to failure for the very reason that Olesha's poetics strongly resist clear-cut solutions and conclusions. Olesha's poetics do not allow his works easily to be classified as gay or gloomy, happy or pessimistic, positive or negative. The elements of optimism and pessimism, alienation and ecstasy all appear in Olesha, but they appear in varying proportions in different works, and in his best works they are in a state of active competition with each other. This highly competitive, even combative relationship between elements of Olesha's works is one of their true hallmarks and a sign of their tremendously dialogical, and not prescriptive, character. When Olesha resorts to positivistic or didactic conclusions, as he does in some of his sketches and dramatic works, the dialogical quality of his poetics collapses, and brings down the level of artistic quality with it.

Except for a few cases, such as *A Strict Youth*, where the work's overall structure is itself poorly defined and there is in fact no real dialogue, the ambiguity and ambivalence that often come from Olesha's intense dialogicality should not be viewed as a shortcoming, as many critics have intimated. To the contrary, Olesha's ambivalence may have extremely creative functions. His many variations on certain basic themes and motifs are an example of a productive offshoot of his inability to come to a final position about certain issues. Furthermore, in combination with his struggles against generic canons, his dialogical ambivalence gives great scope to the reader for fashioning meaning and structure from his works. As we have seen with respect to *Envy* and *No Day without a Line*, one salient feature of these works is that they contain a multiplicity of textual structures and meanings that the reader may deduce from them. This feature does not mean that one reading is as good as the next. The constant and fundamental error made by so many of Olesha's critics is that they claim to have found his final word in places where there is none. Any reading of *Envy* and *No Day without a Line* or the early stories that does not take into account the fact that Olesha gives not one but several words of roughly equal weight will obscure their essentially dialogical character.

One of the most powerful motives behind Olesha's worldview and his poetics is his perception of the mutability of both the objects of the physical world and of people. His frequent showing of objects from contrasting far and near or light and dark perspectives is a manifestation of this motive. Olesha's propensity for playing variations on a given theme, motif, or character—one of the dominant features of his works when considered together—also stems in part from this perception. His sense of the world's changeability also helps to explain why he is often so ambivalent and why he seldom arrives at definitive answers to the questions he poses. There is another, even more important reason for this: Olesha visualizes problems and conflicts not in terms of answers and resolutions but in terms of the dialogical oppositions and carnivalistic juxtapositions that permeate his best works.

4 /
Poetics as Counterpoetics

ONE intriguing miniature sketch in *No Day without a Line* appears to contain something like a parable of Olesha's literary career. The parable is told in the form of an extended metaphor in which his career is compared with a "metaphor shop" the writer once had: "In my old age I opened a metaphor shop. . . . I was convinced that I would get rich. Indeed, I had a marvelous supply of metaphors. Once a fire almost took place in the shop because of one of them" (522).

The fire was started by a metaphor in which it was said that a "puddle lay under a tree like a gypsy." Another metaphor, "when you eat cherries, it seems as though it is raining" (522), turned out to be so successful that sparrows came who wanted to pick at the cherries:

> And thus I supposed that I would get rich on my metaphors.
> However, the shoppers did not buy the expensive ones; for the most part metaphors like "pale as death" were sold. . . . But these were cheap goods, and I could not even make ends meet. When I noticed that I myself was already taking to such expressions as "making ends meet," I decided to close the shop. (522)

The most fascinating thing about this miniature is that it appears to contain Olesha's own interpretation of what went wrong with his literary career and what led to his fall from the upper echelons of Russian literature. The sparrows who came to pick at the cherries are undoubtedly the critics who in the early 1930s began to react harshly against *Envy* and the brilliant stories of the *Cherry Stone* cycle and urged Olesha to change his writing style and even his whole outlook on life. When Olesha began to produce cheap metaphors, that is, stories of second-rate quality, they were bought up. His newspaper articles, film scenarios, and sketches of the middle of the 1930s and 1940s were mostly sold and published, but they were not of sufficient stature to provide the author with a living or a reputation. Consequently, the author closed his shop, or ceased to attempt to write serious fiction at all. The basic metaphor of this short sketch in which metaphors stand for stories is symptomatic of the whole literary credo as expressed in *No Day without a Line* in which Olesha equates metaphor with or even substitutes it for fiction itself.

Olesha is the first to tell us about his triumphs and the first to let us know that he has failed. He is the first to praise his own work and the first to disparage it. In *No Day without a Line*, as noted, he calls *Envy* a book that will "live for the ages" (451). In another place he states that the novel contains "too many similes and metaphors. . . . One should write more dryly, more sparingly, more simply."[1] This vacillation between confidence in himself and self-effacement indicates that not only is he ambivalent about the characters, events and themes of his work but he is also unable to decide what is best about it. Perhaps this indecision on Olesha's part is responsible for his having achieved much less than what his early successes promised. His characteristic ambivalence, a positive stimulus for the dialogical quality of his best works, may, therefore, also be partly responsible for his inability to accomplish as much as he might have. There are, of course, other factors that should be taken into account.

In assessing Olesha's long absence from the highest ranks of his contemporary Russian writers it would be unfair to underestimate the tremendous social, political, and ideological pressures that were brought to bear on him and on other writers of his time. Some of his favorite themes and characters were literally taken away from him. The eroticism that peaks in and out of some of his early works simply becomes taboo by the middle of the 1930s. Zhdanov's promulgation of the heroization of literature that took place in conjunction with the adoption of Socialist realism in 1934 robbed Olesha of one of his favorite character types, the outcast or the bum. According to Zhdanov's formula, writers were discouraged from writing about little people and their lives and encouraged to concern themselves with the great deeds of great heroes.[2] Without a character such as the beggar he had planned to write a novel about, Olesha's carnivalistic double pair, big shot/bum, was deprived of one of its members.

Bereft of his most congenial characters and themes, Olesha came to feel that he was out of touch with the prevailing literary tastes and demands of the 1930s. Contrary to myth, he did not give up the battle to write but continued to struggle with what turned out to be the artificial and limiting theme of Soviet youth in his plays and film scenarios and even in his short stories.

With the benefit of hindsight it is possible to see that part of Olesha's problem may have had to do with paths not taken. Despite the fact that his later children's works, such as the story "About the Fox" (*O lise*) (1948) and the film cartoon *A Little Girl at the Circus* (1958), are not particularly distinguished,[3] Olesha seems to have had considerable potential for becoming a major author of children's literature. He has a knack for creating vivid realized metaphors, such as the exploding cabbage heads in *Three Fat Men*. He also has an enormous talent for evoking a holiday atmosphere that is prominent in many of his works. When he wishes to, he is able to construct the sort of suspenseful plot needed in a children's story. His narrative techniques would appear to be especially appropriate for children's literature. The intimate relationship between reader and narrator that Olesha creates in his short works is singularly suitable for children's stories. Furthermore, as may be seen throughout his major works such as *Envy*, the stories from the *Cherry Stone* cycle, and *No Day without a Line*, he is particularly resourceful in the creation of childlike points of view. Above all, he has exactly the kind of whimsical imagination required of a children's writer.

It is hard to understand why Olesha abandoned children's literature for so long after his auspicious debut in *Three Fat Men*. It is even more puzzling when one takes into account the fact that he took a special interest in children's literature and counted among his favorite writers some famous for their children's literature. He is particularly fond of Mark Twain, who he considers to be one of the great writers of world literature, and whose children's works, such as *Tom Sawyer* and *The Prince and the Pauper*, he rates with the greatest works of children's literature.[4]

Olesha also had several contemporaries who he held in great esteem and who serve as models of writers engaged in both adult and children's literature. Mayakovsky, who inspired Olesha's unabashed awe, is the author of several children's poems.[5] Zoshchenko, another friend who produced a number of stories for children, turned like Daniel Kharms to children's literature as a haven when the times made it difficult to pursue the themes and techniques of his adult works. During the middle of the 1930s, when Olesha's concern with the dilemmas of the Soviet intelligentsia was no longer on the list of officially favored subjects, it seems logical that he might have further applied his talents to children's literature. But Olesha rarely did what was logical or expected; instead he took upon himself what turned out to be a Sisyphean task of attempting to portray the new Soviet youth. With the wisdom of hindsight it is tempting to say that he might have served himself and his readers better had he written more for youth instead of about youth.

Even if Olesha's potential was not fully realized, and even if some of his lesser works are mediocre at best, his legacy is a tremendously significant and enduring one. *Envy* remains not just a classic of the late 1920s but a genuine and permanent metafictional masterpiece of its own kind, one that continues to provoke spirited popular and critical attention. Perhaps Shklovsky's claim that in *Three Fat Men* Olesha has created the fairy tale anew is no exaggeration.[6] For *Three Fat Men* has captured the imagination of the public in a way that few other works in Russian literature of the Soviet period have. Olesha's stories, which are sometimes thought to suffer by comparison with *Envy*, in some cases actually attain a level of artistic perfection that has rarely been achieved in Soviet Russian short fiction. Finally, it has been interesting to observe that his atonement for so many years of squandered talent, *No Day without a Line*, may turn out to be his most influential work.

The influence of *No Day without a Line* is clearly perceptible not only in Valentin Kataev's *My Diamond Wreath* but in his other memoirs as well: *The Holy Well (Sviatoi kolodets)* (1966), *The Grass of Oblivion (Trava zabven'ia)* (1967), and *The Shattered Life, or the Magic Horn of Oberon (Razbitaia zhizn', ili Volshebnyi rog Oberona)* (1972) all bear the unmistakable imprint of *No Day without a Line*. In *The Shattered Life* Kataev tries to bring back his experience of childhood in much the same fashion Olesha does in *No Day without a Line*, and in *The Grass of Oblivion*, Kataev openly admits at one point that he is writing in the style of Olesha in *No Day without a Line*.[7] In all likelihood, *No Day without a Line* will also have an impact on the way in which other Russian authors write their memoirs.

In both his life and his art Olesha constantly remakes and makes up the world for himself. This process leads to the creation of a number of alternate realms and systems that display his own eccentric stamp and that are to varying degrees unorthodox or extraordinary. Childhood is so appealing to him both because it is a realm where first perceptions are always out of the ordinary and because it forms a reality outside of the present. The world of the carnival is so attractive both because it dramatizes the spectacular and because it forms a world outside of the everyday. Olesha dwells so much in childhood and the carnival because they both replace the usual routine of adult life with their own conventions.

Olesha's poetics give the impression of a certain literary "lawlessness," because he so often remakes genres and forms so that they produce alternate structures that are particularly suited to him. His poetics are so much the product of a struggle against established systems and conventions that they might even be called a kind of counterpoetics. Even his inferior works—*Cardinal Questions*, *Walter*, and "The Komsomol Organizer" (*Komsorg*) (1936)—highlight the essential character of his poetics, if only negatively. For when he writes in the way that others wanted or expected him to, the results are only a faint, sometimes even distorted, echo of his real capabilities. Olesha, who prides himself on being able to name things differently, who writes in a "new" way, and whose poetics are largely a counterpoetics, is not successful as a conformist. He is convincing when he creates other realities but not when he imitates others' realities.

The nature of Olesha's relationships with other writers also illustrates the fundamental qualities of his poetics. In all of these relationships he modifies, adapts, and reconstructs elements and techniques found in other writers according to the rules of his own system. When he returns to his youth, he does so not as Proust did, but in his own fashion. When he "borrows" a landscape from Wells, the result is not a copy of Wells but something of his own creation. If Olesha's Kavalerov and Ivan Babichev put the reader in mind of Dostoevsky's underground men,[8] then it is also apparent that their frivolity and eccentricity belong to him and not to Dostoevsky. The same may be said about his literary carnival, which is both more overt and often more lighthearted than Dostoevsky's. In Dostoevsky aspects of the carnival appear in a greatly transformed aspect that is deprived of any sort of gaiety or celebration.

Each of Olesha's handful of masterpieces gives the impression of literature created anew, because his poetics are so thoroughly grounded in his own eccentric vision and in a struggle against standard practices and norms. Even though his poetics are largely a counterpoetics, they are remarkably systematic and consistent within themselves. He constantly seeks to re-create not only the world around him but also the literary structures with which he depicts it. Outside of the relatively superficial imitations of Olesha's treatment of sport, the essential qualities of his work appear difficult to emulate. Perhaps this has to do with the fact that he is a persistent recaster and reshaper of familiar forms and conventions. He is also so elusive and so little susceptible to imitation because his literary dialogues are so thoroughly ambivalent and so imbued with a special carnivalistic sensibility of his own genesis. Olesha should not be judged, however, by the success or scope of his few followers. It is the remarkable intersection of his own eccentric carnival, his own distinctive dialogicality, and his own special estrangement that constitutes his essence and the core of his original contribution to Russian literature.

Notes

Introduction: Life and Carnival

1. In *Vospominaniia o Yurii Oleshe* (1975), comps. O. Suok-Olesha and E. Pel'son, Ovchinnikov calls Olesha a "knight of perfection" (54). Virtually all of the reminiscences about Olesha in this book are highly laudatory of him. Slavin does note that he had a sharp tongue and could annihilate an opponent in a verbal battle (12). Because of this and Olesha's sarcasm, Lepeshinskaia wonders whether "one could call Yury Karlovich kind [*dobryi*]" (133). Livanov, on the other hand, is one of those who considered Olesha to be a "magician" and "a fairy-tale gnome" (126). Belinkov is the major proponent of the notion that he was a person of low and mean character and consistently tries to show him in such a light in *Sdacha i gibel' sovetskogo intelligenta: Yurii Olesha* (1976).

2. For example, in *The Invisible Land: A Study of the Artistic Imagination of Iurii Olesha* (1970), Beaujour cites Olesha's "refusal to debase art to the level of immediate social command" (196).

3. Kazakevich, in *Vospominaniia o Yurii Oleshe*, comps. O. Suok-Olesha and E. Pel'son, 293–94.

4. Belinkov repeats this thesis many times throughout *Sdacha i gibel' sovetskogo intelligenta: Yurii Olesha*. Perhaps Belinkov's most damaging point against Olesha concerns a talk the latter gave (excerpted in "*Velikoe narodnoe iskusstvo*," *Literaturnaia gazeta*, 20 March 1936) in which he criticizes Dmitry Shostakovich for writing music that is lacking in melody and concern for the common man. Belinkov considers Olesha's remarks a form of betrayal, because in 1936, under Stalin, negative criticism of an artist's work could be used as grounds for destroying the individual.

5. Rosengrant's introduction to his 1979 translation of Olesha's *No Day without a Line* is one of the best sources in English for information about Olesha's life. He mentions Olesha's gold medal (12).

6. Starostin, in *Vospominaniia*, comps. Suok-Olesha and Pel'son, 58, writes that when Olesha and he first met, Olesha quizzed him about his knowledge of Odessan soccer. Olesha began by mentioning that he had played with Bogemsky on their gymnasium team.

7. This is from *Ni dnia bez strochki* in Olesha, *Izbrannoe* (1974), 414–15. Subsequent citations to *Izbrannoe* will be indicated in the text in parentheses. Translations from Russian in this book are my own.

8. Pertsov, in *Vospominaniia*, comps. Suok-Olesha and Pel'son, 249.

9. Brumberg and Brumberg, ibid., 147.

10. See Starostin's *Vstrechi na futbol'noi orbite* (1980), 129–30, and his article "*Ya pomniu*," in *Yunost'* no. 5 (May 1983): 109.

11. Nikulin, in *Vospominaniia*, comps. Suok-Olesha and Pel'son, 69.

12. These facts have been compiled from *Vospominaniia*, comps. Suok-Olesha and Pel'son, *Ni dnia bez strochki, Izbrannoe* (1974), and an autobiographical note by Olesha, "Avtobiografii 3,"in *Sovetskie pisateli*, 517–19.

13. Gerasimov, in *Vospominaniia*, comps. Suok-Olesha and Pel'son, 101.

14. Olesha, "*Avtobiografii*,"517.

15. Aborsky, in *Vospominaniia*, comps. Suok-Olesha and Pel'son, 200–201.

16. Lidin, ibid., 170.

17. See Babel's stories about Odessa in *Konarmiia, Odesskie rasskazy, P'esy* (1957, 1965). These stories have been translated into English by Andrew R. MacAndrew in Isaac Babel, *Lyubka the Cossack and Other Stories* (New York: New American Library, 1963), 10–106.

18. See especially p. 357 in *Izbrannoe* (1974).

19. See *Ni dnia bez strochki*, ibid., where Olesha writes, "I wrote like Igor' Severianin, in a mannered, silly, extravagant way. . . . But look, I did see something nevertheless!" (431).

20. This is quoted from E. I. Rozanova's dissertation written at the State University of Odessa, "Proza Yuriia Oleshi" (1976), 39.

21. Ibid.

22. This poem was published in *Bomba* no. 11 (Odessa, 1917): 10. It is quoted here from Olesha's archive in Moscow at Tsentral'nyi Gosudarstvennyi Arkhiv Literatury i Iskusstva (TsGALI), fond 358, opis; 1, "Yu. K. Olesha. *Stikhotvoreniia, 1917–1921*." Here too the dominant colors of Olesha's Odessan palette are green and blue. The museum is "all blue" (*ves' sinii*), and the "boulevard goes off into the distance like a green road" (*ukhodit vdal' zelenoiu dorogoi*).

23. *Vospominaniia*, comps. Suok-Olesha and Pel'son, 25.

24. Ibid., 176–77.

25. Ibid., 172.

26. Kataev, *Almaznyi moi venets. Povesti* (1981), 94.

27. Ibid., 192–93.

28. Kataev masterfully draws out the tale of Olesha and druzhok over pp. 106–8, 129, 134–35, ibid. The girl's nickname for Olesha was "*slonenok*" (little elephant). The man she eventually wound up with was a poet whom Kataev dubs "the lame" (*kolchenogii*).

29. Ibid., 104–5.

30. See, for example, ibid., 128.

31. Ibid., 300.

32. Smeliakov, in *Vospominaniia*, comps. Suok-Olesha and Pel'son, 243–44, describes how he accompanied Olesha and his wife on this escapade.

33. Ozerov, ibid., 241.

34. In addition to the material that was published posthumously in *Ni dnia bez strochki*, Olesha left unfinished numerous fragments of plays, such as *The Death of Sand* (*Smert' Zanda*), which is discussed in chapter 3, as well as at least one play, *Bilbao*, that was virtually complete.

35. The foregoing is a synthesis of the many reminiscences by Olesha's colleagues and friends in *Vospominaniia*, comps. Suok-Olesha and Pel'son. Komardenkov describes the Georgian restaurant Olesha frequented (39). Aborsky is one of several people to note the abundance of story plots Olesha had at his disposal (194). Lidin describes Olesha's inability to manage his time (170).

36. Slavin mentions "the false Chisel" in *Vospominaniia*, comps. Suok-Olesha and Pel'son, 9. This verse is quoted from Ovchinnikov, ibid., 46. It is from the poem *Popy v bane, a rabochie okolo bani*, which may be found in Olesha's *Saliut. Stikhi* (Moscow: Gudok, 1927).

37. The play *Igra v plakhu* (1922, 1934) is discussed in chapter 2. Shklovsky is one of the few who finds connections between Olesha's verse satire and his prose, but he does so in a somewhat enigmatic fashion, as the following quotation from his introduction to Olesha's *Izbrannoe* (1974) indicates: " 'The Chisel' was a journalist. The great lyricist Olesha remained a journalist" (7). Gladkov is substantially correct when he states that there is virtually no connection between Olesha's satirical verse and his prose in *Vospominaniia*, comps. Suok-Olesha and Pel'son, 268. Pertsov points out in *My zhivem vpervye. O tvorchestve Yuriia Oleshi* (1976), 79, that the only links between *Envy* and Olesha's satirical feuilletons are superficial and consist of some individual details and metaphors.

38. See Ovchinnikov, in *Vospominaniia*, comps. Suok-Olesha and Pel'son, 46.

39. See, for example Slavin, in *Vospominaniia*, comps. Suok-Olesha and Pel'son, 8, and Ovchinnikov, ibid., 43, 54.

40. See Belinkov, *Sdacha i gibel' sovetskogo intelligenta*, 70–71.

41. An excellent description of the way these writers worked together at *The Whistle* is Paustovsky's "*Chetvertaia polosa*," *Sbornik vospominanii ob I. Il'fe i E. Petrove* (1963). Paustovsky calls Olesha, Babel', Bulgakov, and Il'f "masters of the oral story" (83).

42. Quoted in Olesha, *Zavist'* (1929), 142. This is from a May edition of *Pravda*. This edition of *Envy* contains excerpts from a wide variety of publications from 1927–28 that demonstrate beyond a doubt that the initial reaction to *Envy* was enthusiastic.

43. See Pertsov, *My zhivem vpervye* (1976), 111, and Barratt, *Yurii Olesha's* "Envy," 6.

44. Polonsky's article, *"Preodolenie* zavisti" (1929), is a good example of an early reassessment of the originally enthusiastic reception. The introduction to Szulkin's Harvard doctoral dissertation "The Artistic Prose of Jurij Karlovich Olesha" (1968), especially pp. 20–28, contains a detailed account of the early critical reception of Olesha's first works, including *Envy*. Szulkin also deals with Olesha's attempts to meet that criticism with his own self-justification.

45. See part 2 of Belinkov's article, *"Poet i tolstiak,"* 101. Belinkov refers to several sources in order to illustrate Andrei Babichev's uneven path through Soviet criticism: Viktor Pertsov, *"O knigakh, vyshedshikh desiat' let tomu nazad,"* *Literaturnaia gazeta*, 26 June 1937; Pertsov, "Yurii Olesha" in Olesha's *Izbrannye sochineniia* (Moscow: Gos. izdat. khudozhestvennaia literatura, 1956), 11; Galanov, *"Mir* Yuriia Oleshi," in Olesha's *Povesti i rasskazy*, 9–10. In both parts of *"Poet i tolstiak,"* Belinkov is much more ambiguous and less harsh in his judgment of Olesha than he is in *Sdacha i gibel'*.

46. See *My zhivem vpervye*, 37–38, where Pertsov discusses Chudakova's *Masterstvo Yuriia Oleshi*.

47. Olesha, *Izbrannoe* (1974), 7.

48. *Sdacha i gibel'*, 482–91.

49. Pertsov, *My zhivem vpervye*, 111; Barratt, *Yurii Olesha's* "Envy," 6.

50. The reviews are mainly of contemporary writers. A list of them may be found in *Russkie sovetskie pisateli. Prozaiki. Bibliograficheskii ukazatel'* (Leningrad: Publichnaia biblioteka im. Saltykova-Shchedrina, 1964), 3: 356.

51. Gladkov does not mention the name of the writer with whom Olesha jousts in *Vospominaniia*, 269.

52. Olesha published *"Iz literaturnykh dnevnikov"* in *Literaturnaia Moskva* (Moscow, 1956), 2: 731, 732. Selections from Olesha's notes were also published in *Sovetskii tsirk* no. 6 (1961): 23–26, *Oktiabr'* no. 7 (1961): 147–69 and no. 8 (1961): 9–11. The first independent book is *Ni dnia bez strochki: Iz zapisnych knizhek* (1965). The differences between this work and the edition of *Ni dnia* published in Olesha's *Izbrannoe* (1974), 341–558, are discussed in chapter 2. Olesha had various names for his book and never seemed to have settled on a single title. Aborsky reports in *Vospominaniia*, 200, that it was to be called "What I Saw on Earth" (*Chto ya videl na zemle*). Gladkov discussed with Olesha the merits and demerits of the title *Words, Words, Words* (*Slova, slova, slova*), as he notes in *Vospominaniia*, 279. Olesha specifically mentions this title in *Ni dnia*, *Izbrannoe* (1974), 445. Slavin believes that the title was going to be *My Novel* (*Moi roman*) (in *Vospominaniia*, 16). Kataev prefers "Saying Goodbye to the World" (*Proshchanie s mirom*), which is

the title of his article in vol. 8 of his *Sobranie sochinenii*, 9 vols. (Moscow: Khudozhestvennaia literatura, 1971), 436–38.

53. *Vospominaniia*, 299. In the final analysis, Mikhail Gromov did most of the work.

54. Shklovsky, *"Struna zvenit v tumane,"* 197.

55. *Avtobiografii* 3: 522–23.

56. Ibid., 523.

57. See Perel', *"Pravoflangovye otechestvennogo futbola"* (1969), 100.

58. See Starostin, *Vstrechi na futbol'noi orbite*, 120. The appearance of *Envy* actually spawned several imitators of Olesha, such as Sergei Bondarin and V. Dmitriev, who wrote some stories about soccer. Chudakova discusses Olesha's influence on these two writers in *Masterstvo Yuriia Oleshi* (1972), 54–55.

59. The articles are *"Na matche,"* Vecherniaia Moskva, 19 September 1936, *"Baski,"* Vecherniaia Moskva, 25 June 1937, and *"Khrustal'nyi kubok,"* Moskovskii bol'shevik, 16 October 1945. In *"Baski"* Olesha describes the match between the Spanish national team and Moscow *Dinamo* in virtually the same terms as he describes the soccer match in *Envy*, when he writes, "It was a holiday."

60. Bakhtin in *Rabelais and His World* (1968), 235, notes that in the carnival "games drew players out of the bounds of the everyday." For a description of folk games as the beginnings of sport see Kharabuga, *"Fizicheskaia kul'tura v srednie veka,"* 36–38.

61. Szulkin notes in "The Artistic Prose of Juriij Karlovich Olesha," 422, Olesha's special ability to see and understand both sides of an issue simultaneously.

62. There is considerable debate over how to attribute the authorship of certain works that have been associated with the names of Bakhtin, V. N. Voloshinov, and P. N. Medvedev. In *Mikhail Bakhtin* (1984), Katerina Clark and Michael Holquist argue persuasively that *Marxism and the Philosophy of Language* (*Marksizm i filosofiia yazyka*) (1929), which has been attributed to V. N. Voloshinov, really belongs to the overall œuvre of Bakhtin. They treat *The Formal Method in Literary Scholarship* (*Formal'nyi metod v literaturovedenii*) (1928), of which Medvedev is elsewhere credited as coauthor, in the same way. See pp. 146–70 for Clark and Holquist's treatment of the problem of the disputed texts.

In the Preface to their translation of *Marxism and the Philosophy of Language* (Cambridge: Harvard University Press, 1986), ix–xii, Ladislav Matejka and I. R. Titunik retain Voloshinov as the author of signature and discuss the numerous problems that arise out of merging all of the works in question under Bakhtin's name.

The whole controversy is greatly complicated by, among other things, the dangers of authorship in the Stalin period, the fact that the three scholars involved collaborated, consulted, and conferred on so many projects of mutual interest, Bakhtin's reluctance officially to clarify the issue in his lifetime, and perhaps even a certain fondness for a tradition of mystification that sometimes manifests itself in Russian letters. It is unlikely that the debate will be resolved in the near future. In any event, the point of this debate has never been to diminish Bakhtin's contribution to modern thought, since Bakhtin was clearly the dominant figure in the circles in which he participated.

63. In *Mikhail Bakhtin* Clark and Holquist often refer to Bakhtin's love of strong tea.

64. Clark and Holquist have shown that outside of his activity in various intellectual circles, and particularly in his later life, Bakhtin kept to himself. Partly because of chronic ill health and partly because of a lack of practicality, he was dependent on his wife, Elena Aleksandrovna Okolovich, for the provision of everyday necessities. This pronounced impracticality, as we have seen above, was also a hallmark of Olesha. Another trait he had in common with Olesha was the difficulty in finishing his work that Clark and Holquist note in several places.

65. Clark and Holquist, *Mikhail Bakhtin,* 27.

66. Clark and Holquist note that Bakhtin was an opponent of canons of all types, ibid., 4.

67. Ibid., 317.

68. Ibid.

69. Shklovsky's famous concept, *ostranenie,* has been translated variously as "estrangement," "making strange," "bestrangement," and "defamiliarization." This last translation was made popular by Stacy in his Shklovskian study *Defamiliarization in Language and Literature* (1977). It has also been adopted by Morson in *The Boundaries of Genre: Dostoevsky's* Diary of a Writer *and the Traditions of Literary Utopia* (1981). The virtue of translating *ostranenie* as "defamiliarization" is twofold. It avoids confusion with uses of the word "estrangement" that have to do with social and psychological states, and it underlines Shklovsky's notion that the task of art is to make unfamiliar things that have become so familiar that they are virtually "automatized" in the viewer-reader's perception of them. See his *"O teorii prozy"* (1929), 13. The terms "estrangement" and "defamiliarization" will be employed here interchangeably with the understanding that the former is a term used only in reference to art and literature.

70. Morson's *Boundaries of Genre* shows how writers such as Dostoevsky, Shklovsky, Zamiatin, and others challenge our preconceptions about fictional and literary genres in such a way as both to transcend the traditional boundaries of these genres and to make us think through and rethink the structure of their works as we read them. Morson's work is the basis for my first chapter called "From Metafiction to Meta-

literature." I have of course in some instances modified Morson's terms and approach to suit my own purposes.

71. Bakhtin describes and defines the phenomenon of carnivalistic literature throughout both *Rabelais and His World* and *Problemy poetiki Dostoevskogo* (1979). More specifically, the treatment of carnivalized literature in this book is based largely on pp. 140–59 of Bakhtin's analysis of Dostoevsky's poetics. This will be discussed in greater detail in the beginning of chapter 2.

72. Bakhtin develops his notion of dialogue throughout most of his work. The major sources used here are in *Problemy poetiki Dostoevskogo* and *The Dialogic Imagination: Four Essays by M. M. Bakhtin* (1981), particularly in the chapter "Discourse in the Novel," 259–422.

Chapter 1. From Metafiction to Metaliterature

1. Shklovsky, *Zoo, or Letters Not about Love,* trans. Richard Sheldon (1971), 23. The translation is from *Zoo, ili Pis'ma ne o liubvi* (Berlin: Helikon Publishing House, 1923). Morson's treatment of *Zoo* in *The Boundaries of Genre* is the starting point for my examination of Shklovsky.

2. In *The Boundaries of Genre,* Morson refers to *War and Peace* as an example of a work that is on the threshold between genres, it is "part novel, and part essay . . . both a novel and 'not a novel' " (51).

3. Ibid., 54.

4. Morson describes the technique of "framing" or "reframing" in the same place.

5. I have discussed Pil'niak's techniques in "Pil'njak's Use of Documents and Pseudo-documents in *Golyj god*" (1982).

6. See Morson, *The Boundaries of Genre,* 134.

7. Morson describes works that the reader may find "doubly encodable" or that the author has "doubly encoded," ibid., 48–51.

8. See the notes to *Tri tolstiaka* by Badikov in Olesha's *Izbrannoe* (1974), 562. The play premiered in 1930. The ballet was first presented with music by V. Oransky in 1935. The music for the opera is by V. Rubin.

9. See Shklovsky in *Vospominaniia,* comps. Suok-Olesha and Pel'son, 300, and Pertsov in *My zhivem vpervye,* 99.

10. Pertsov writes in *My Zhivem vpervye,* 99, that the Suok family were Odessans of Austrian background.

11. See Olesha's *Ni dnia bez strochki, Izbrannoe* (1974), 410.

12. In *My zhivem vpervye,* 98, Pertsov notes this connection between Olesha and Grin.

13. *Ni dnia bez strochki, Izbrannoe* (1974), 504.

14. In the same work, pp. 5–6, Olesha writes that he was brought up first on European rather than Russian literature.

15. Yury Olesha, *Complete Stories and Three Fat Men* (1979), 257–61.

16. See A. and D. Anderson in the afterword to Olesha's *Complete Stories and Three Fat Men*, 260.

17. A. Anderson makes an especially clever translation of this name as *"Undeuxtrois."*

18. In *Paths Through the Forest: A Biography of the Brothers Grimm* (1971), 58–59, M. B. Peppard discusses the question of cruelty in the tales recorded by the Brothers Grimm. He notes that these tales are popular in Russia (40).

19. See Szulkin, "The Artistic Prose of Jurij Karlovich Olesha," 173. Szulkin discusses the relationship between *Three Fat Men* and *The Tempest* in some detail, 173–76.

20. Ibid., 174.

21. Bulgakov, *Sbornik rasskazov*, 155.

22. Sokol discusses Chukovsky's battles with the "leftist pedologists," who included Nadezhda Krupskaya, in *Russian Poetry for Children*, 9–10.

23. *My zhivem vpervye*, 111.

24. See Struve, *Russian Literature under Lenin and Stalin, 1917–1951* (1971), 106, a revised version of his *Soviet Russian Literature* (Norman: University of Oklahoma Press, 1951).

25. Ibid.

26. See Maguire, *Red Virgin Soil: Soviet Literature in the 1920s*, 344.

27. Berczynski, "Kavalerov's Monologue in *Envy:* A Baroque Soliloquy" (1971), 376.

28. Ibid., 376–77.

29. Croft discusses the cinematic technique Olesha uses in describing the soccer match in "Charlie Chaplin and Olesha's *Envy*" (1978), 530.

30. See Solov'ev, "Gulliver v strane velikanov" (1974), 164.

31. Chukovsky, *Chukokala*, 24.

32. This has been quoted in Shklovsky's introduction to Olesha's *Izbrannoe* (1974), 8–9.

33. See Glan, in *Vospominanii*, comps. Suok-Olesha and Pel'son, 290.

34. In *The Artist and the Creative Act: A Study of Jurij Olesha's Novel Zavist'* (1984), 126–28, Ingdahl believes that Olesha's unmasking of his imagery is a way of making his work useful and an act of self-justification. It seems more likely that Olesha's method derives from the highly self-conscious, Sternian, Shklovskian poetics he cultivates on so many levels. Also, Olesha was fond of drawing attention to his own cleverness and savoring a successful simile or metaphor with the reader.

35. See Shklovsky, *"Poeziia i proza v kinematografii," Poetika kino*, 137–42.

36. B. Kazansky, "*Priroda kino,*" 90, 93–94.

37. See Shklovsky's "*Poeziia i proza v kinomatografii,*" 142, and Olesha's film scenario, "*Kardinal'nye voprosy*" (1935), 45.

38. Olesha, "*Kardinal'nye voprosy,*" 46.

39. *My zhivem vpervye,* 215. Pertsov discusses Olesha's dramatization of *The Idiot* in relation to Dostoevsky's novel on pp. 192–224. Also, parts of Olesha's script are quoted on pp. 205, 207–14, 217.

40. See Olesha and A. Macheret, *Val'ter* (1937), 14–45. This scenario was produced as the film *Bolotnye soldaty* (*Swamp Soldiers*) in 1938.

41. See Olesha's *P'esy. Stat'i o teatre i dramaturgii* (1968), 68. Subsequent references to Olesha's plays in this work will be indicated by the letter "P" and the relevant page number in parentheses.

42. Quoted in the unattributed notes to Olesha, *Tri tolstiaka* in *P'esy* (1968), 382.

43. Olesha, "*Moia rabota s MKHAT,*" *P'esy,* 323.

44. Both Chernova's objections and Olesha's reply are contained in Olesha, "*Pis'mo komsomol'ke* Chernovoi" (1935), 160.

45. Ibid.

46. Pertsov, *My zhivem vpervye,* 63.

47. See Konstantin Rudnitsky's *Rezhisser Meierkhol'd,* 438. Meyerhold talked with Olesha about the experiences of the actor, Mikhail Chekhov, in Europe. Chekhov is a model for the play's heroine, Elena Goncharova, who also visits Europe.

48. See V. E. Meyerhold, *Stat'i, pis'ma, rechi, besedy* 2: 249.

49. Struve, *Russian Literature under Lenin and Stalin, 1917–1953,* 236.

50. See Gladkov, *Vospominaniia,* 280.

51. Shklovsky, "*Struna zvenit v tumane,*" 205.

52. Compare *Ni dnia bez strochki. Iz zapisnykh knizhek* (1965), 208, with *Ni dnia bez strochki* in Olesha's *Izbrannoe* (1974), 486. What is left out in the later edition is Olesha's characterization of Tolstoy's description of mowing in *Anna Karenina* as "preaching gymnastics." Perhaps the editors felt that this remark did not reflect well on Olesha's literary judgment. The 1974 edition tends to include certain items that might be construed as controversial, such as a description of how the Tsar spoke to Olesha (402), presumably in a crowd, and a sympathetic description of some foreign interventionist soldiers in the civil war in Odessa (425). In general, the later edition of *No Day without a Line* conveys the dark side of Olesha's life, including references to his alcoholism, more fully than the earlier one.

53. Quoted from Makhumdov, "*Zametki o tvorcheskom kontekste,*" 15. This is part of a letter from Zoshchenko to Olesha from the personal archive of Olga Suok-Olesha. The letter appeared here in full for the first

time and was prepared for publication by Badikov. Zoshchenko's remarks are clearly part of an ongoing dialogue between the two writers about Olesha's "searches for form" (14).

54. Shklovsky, "*Struna zvenit v tumane*," 200.

55. Ibid., 201.

56. See the introduction to V. V. Rozanov, *Izbrannoe* (New York: Chekhov Publishing House, 1956), 46.

57. Beaujour, "Proust-*Envy*: Fiction and Autobiography in the Works of Iurii Olesha," 130–31.

58. Ibid., 128.

59. Ibid., 128–29.

60. Morson, *The Boundaries of Genre*, 59.

61. Ibid., 62.

62. Ibid., 53.

Chapter 2. Variations on the Carnival

1. The discussion of Bakhtin and subsequent treatment of *Envy* are based on my article "Olesha's *Envy* and the Carnival" (1984), 179–89.

2. Bakhtin sets forth his concept of carnivalistic or carnivalized literature in *Problemy poetiki Dostoevskogo*, 140–59.

3. Ibid., 141–42.

4. Ibid., 146–47.

5. Ibid., 147.

6. Ibid., 143–44.

7. Ibid., 145.

8. Ibid.

9. Bakhtin deals with the problem of the carnival and Dostoevsky's works throughout *Problemy poetiki Dostoevskogog*. Here I am referring especially to pp. 147, 168–70.

10. *Igra v plakhu* was originally published in *Trudiashchii mir* no. 1 (Kharkov, 1922): 24–43. Subsequently it was reprinted in *30 dnei* no. 5 (1934): 35–48.

11. As Beaujour points out in *The Invisible Land: A Study of the Artistic Imagination of Iurii Olesha*, Olesha's verse gives the play a "genteel and un-Soviet tone" (112).

12. See Bakhtin, *Problemy poetiki Dostoevskogo*, 148.

13. Burke, *Popular Culture in Early Modern Europe*, 185.

14. Quoted in Makhmudov, "*Zametki o tvorcheskom kontekste*," 14. As noted in chapter 1, the full text of the letter is on pp. 14–15. Zoshchenko's remark is more than just friendly encouragement. Zoshchenko, known for his honesty and directness, adds parenthetically that his enthusiasm does not extend to Olesha's plays.

15. Barratt, *Yurii Olesha's* "Envy," 60.
16. Beaujour points out in a note on p. 76 of *The Invisible Land* that Olesha is unconcerned with the medical accuracy of his portrayal of color blindness.
17. Ibid., 16.
18. See Russell's article "Olesha's 'The Cherry Stone,' " 90.
19. Although virtually all critics have noticed Olesha's interest in optical perspective, Nils Åke Nilsson has made the most thorough examination of this question in his articles "Through the Wrong End of Binoculars" (1973) and "A Hall of Mirrors: Nabokov and Olesha" (1969). Olesha's use of optical perspective in *Envy* will be discussed.
20. As Bakhtin observes in *Problemy poetiki Dostoevskogo*, 142, various types of profanation, including blasphemies and obscenities, are integral features of the carnival.
21. Olesha, *"Zametki dramaturga," P'esy* (1968): 295.
22. This is how Lunacharsky characterizes Andrei in *"Zagovor chuvstv,"* 420.
23. Olesha, *"Avtor o svoei p'ese," P'esy* (1968): 261.
24. See Panchenko, *"Problema garmonicheskoi lichnosti v romane Yu. Oleshi* Zavist' *i ego dramaticheskom variante* Zagovor chuvstv," 38.
25. This draft will be discussed in detail in relation to *Envy*. Ingdahl deserves the credit for having brought the draft to light in *The Artist and the Creative Act: A Study of Jurij Olesha's Novel* Zavist', 89–90.
26. See P. Markov, in *Vospominaniia o Yurii Oleshe*, 109.
27. A striking exception is Ronald D. LeBlanc's article "The Soccer Match in *Envy"* (1988) 55–71. In a note on p. 67, LeBlanc in effect rejects my reading in "Olesha's *Envy* and the Carnival" of the soccer match as a culmination of the novel's overall carnivalistic tenor. LeBlanc finds that the ambiguity of the match's outcome enhances the novel's general ambiguity. His article also contains some illuminating comparisons with Andrei Sinyavsky's *The Trial Begins*. Perhaps LeBlanc's most interesting and original insights have to do with his characterization of Volodya Makarov in relation to the heroes of Russian epics and the plots of Stalinist fiction on pp. 60–61.
28. Bakhtin, *Problemy poetiki Dostoevskogo*, 145.
29. Ibid., 146.
30. See Peter Burke's *Popular Culture in Early Modern Europe*, 185.
31. According to Burke, of the three major themes of the carnival, "food, sex, and violence, food was the most obvious" (ibid., 186).
32. Kazimiera Ingdahl, *The Artist and the Creative Act*, 89.
33. This is my own translation from Ingdahl's *The Artist and the Creative Act*, 89–90. The original is located in Olesha's archive in TsGALI, fond 358, *delo* 161.
34. Ibid., 90.

35. Ibid., 90–91. Also, Bakhtin analyzes the Mennipean and carnivalistic features of "Bobok" in Problemy poetiki Dostoevskogo, 167–71.

36. Proffer's article "On The Master and Margarita" (1973) analyzes the relationship of Bulgakov's novel to carnivalistic literature. It is conceivable that Olesha and Bulgakov, who were in contact with each other during the 1920s when they worked together at The Whistle, might have had discussions that touched on carnivalistic literature. As indicated in my introduction, the writers at The Whistle talked among themselves on a wide and diverse range of subjects. At this point, however, I know of no evidence to indicate that Olesha and Bulgakov ever spoke with each other specifically about this topic.

37. Although Burke's description of the carnival differs in many details from that of Bakhtin, he too believes that the carnival's underlying structure is based on paired oppositions, particularly carnival and Lent and carnival and everyday (Popular Culture in Early Modern Europe, 188).

38. The record of this game may be found in Esenin's Moskovskii futbol (1974), 85–86. Although they lost to both the Moscow combined side and to the Pishcheviki club, the German side was considered to be a strong one. Volodya Makarov's eager anticipation of seeing Getzke is probably a reflection of this. During the 1920s matches played by select city teams against each other, and especially against foreign sides, were considered to be the most important of the season. At this time the foreign teams that the Soviets competed with were primarily workers' clubs, although they also occasionally played combined and national sides from the bourgeois countries.

39. Olesha, Ni dnia bez strochki, Izbrannoe (1974), 416–17.

40. Burke, Popular Culture in Early Modern Europe, 184–85.

41. Ibid., 187.

42. This is the view of Piper in "Iurii Olesha's Zavist': An Interpretation" (1970), 41.

43. See Olesha, P'esy (1968), 89. As noted, this ending changes the original one in which Kavalerov turns on Ivan and kills him instead of Andrei.

44. Bakhtin, Problemy poetiki Dostoegovsko, 197.

45. The score of the match that actually took place between the Moscow and German teams, 4 to 1 in favor of Moscow, suggests that the Germans probably scored a single goal in the first half (as also happens in Envy), only to yield four unanswered goals in the second half, thus allowing themselves to be routed.

46. See Polonsky's "Preodolenie Zavisti," 202, and Harkins' "Theme of Sterility in Olesha's Envy" (1966), especially 448. Pertsov makes an exception to the negative appraisals of Markarov in My zhivem vpervye, 128–37.

47. For example, Piper examines the ways in which the major characters represent various projections of Olesha's own personality in "Iurii Olesha's *Zavist'*," 28–29.

48. See Olesha, *Ni dnia bez strochki, Izbrannoe* (1974), 416.

49. Struve calls Valya "earthy" in *Russian Literature under Stalin and Lenin, 1917–1953,* 109. Harkins, on the other hand, calls her "ethereal" in "The Theme of Sterility in Olesha's *Envy*," 456.

50. In *Yurii Olesha's "Envy,"* Barratt has shown that Getzke's name probably comes from the German word "Götzke," which means idol, or false deity (35). Olesha's depiction of Getzke suggests that he is indeed something of a false idol. Nevertheless, it is characteristic of Olesha that he should also show Getzke in a more sympathetic light, even though he is clearly a minor character.

Chapter 3. The Poetics of Dialogue

1. In *Russian Literature under Lenin and Stalin, 1917–1953,* especially 239 and 242, Struve is one of the first to note that Olesha's dialogues are carried out primarily with himself.

2. Bakhtin, *Problemy poetiki Dostoevskogo,* 138.

3. In *The Russian Revolutionary Novel: Turgenev to Pasternak* (1982), Richard Freeborn finds that one of the most interesting things about *Envy* is "its statement of the issues as an equation of *pro and contra*" (156).

4. See Shklovsky, "*Iskusstvo kak priem,*" 14.

5. Sorokin, *Tolstoy in Prerevolutionary Russian Criticism* (1979), 26. It is somewhat surprising that in his attempt to build a typology of narrative techniques Boris Uspensky deals specifically with multiple points of view in *A Poetics of Composition* (1973), 89–97, and constantly refers to Tolstoy but does not take note of the kind of narrative stance found in *Childhood.*

6. As Berczynski notes in "Kavalerov's Monologue in *Envy:* A Baroque Soliloquy," "stylistic unity is not sacrificed for the sake of the narrational scheme" (375).

7. Chudakova, *Masterstvo Yuriia Oleshi,* 23.

8. Ibid., 23–24.

9. Ibid., 24.

10. In *My zhivem vpervye: O tvorchestve Yuriia Oleshi,* 181, Pertsov believes that "Liompa" is "the most perfect and most tragic" of Olesha's stories.

11. In "Yury Olesha's Three Ages of Man: A Close Reading of 'Liompa' " (1980), Barratt discusses the difficulty inherent in reading this story.

12. See ibid., 599.

13. As Szulkin points out in his article "Modes of Perception in Jurij Olesha's *'Liompa'* " (1968), 309, the absence of political and ideological elements raises the level of the story's universality.

14. Barratt, "Yury Olesha's Three Ages of Man," 610.

15. Ibid., 611–12.

16. See ibid., 613–14. As is evident from note 10 above, Pertsov also finds "*Liompa*" to be tragic.

17. Bakhtin sets out his notion of dialogical structure in *Problemy poetiki Dostoevskogo*, 49.

18. Barratt describes this juxtaposition in "Yury Olesha's Three Ages of Man" (606).

19. See Ingdahl's article "Life/Death Dichotomy in Jurij Olesha's Short Story *'Liompa'* " (1982), 158. As Ingdahl points out, the words of the story "*V mire bylo yabloko*" ("In the beginning there was an apple") are an allusion to the beginning of the Gospel according to John: "*V mire bylo slovo*" ("In the beginning was the word"). In Ingdahl's interpretation "the description of the apple contains allusions to the Bibical paradise myth, where it functions as a symbol of fertility and death" (193).

20. Ibid., 164.

21. In *My zhivem vpervye* Pertsov finds this irony to be "especially terrible, because the author has placed it in the lips of a child" (188).

22. Bakhtin, *Rabelais and His World*, 52–53.

23. As Beaujour notes in "Proust-*Envy*: Fiction and Autobiography in the works of Olesha," 127, Olesha had a stepson, Igor, who committed suicide by jumping out of a window in front of both Olesha and his mother, Olga Suok-Olesha. In a note on p. 133 of the same article Beaujour points out that Igor's cousin, Vsevolod Bagritsky, writes about this episode in his book *Dnevniki, pis'ma, stikhi* (1964), 48. Olesha mentions neither Igor nor his wife in *No Day without a Line*. Interestingly, the Oleshas seem to have taken something like a parental interest in Vsevolod Bagritsky, for he reports on p. 36 that they bought him a suit. Olesha was the brother-in-law of Vsevolod's father, Eduard. The younger Bagritsky's book contains several references to Olesha, including one on p. 57 about how other writers envied Olesha for his success.

24. Harkins notes the connection between "Liompa" and *No Day without a Line* in "*No Day without a Line*: The World of Iurii Olesha" (1984), 100.

25. Brumberg and Brumberg, in *Vospominaniia*, 146.

26. Ibid., 177.

27. Olesha, "*Rech' na I Vsesoiuznom s'ezde sovetskikh pisatelei*," *P'esy* (1968), 324.

28. This is what Bondarin calls Olesha in his memoir about him in "*Vstrechi so sverstnikom*," *Gvozd' vinograda* (Moscow: Sovetskii pisatel', 1964), 175.

29. See Kataev, "*Proshchanie s mirom,*" 437.

30. See Olesha, "*O malen'kikh p'esakh,*" *P'esy*, 291. This article was originally published in *30 dnei* no. 8 (1933): 64–65.

31. As Beaujour points out in a note on p. 107 of *The Invisible Land*, "*Chernyi chelovek*" was published in *30 dnei* no. 6 (1932): 27–31, and "*Otryvok iz p'esy Smert' Zanda*" appeared in *Literaturnaia gazeta* (19 October 1930.

32. Ibid., 109.

33. In examining "The Cherry Stone" Harkins writes in "The Philosophical Tales of Jurij Olesha" that "a miraculous synthesis of technology and life" (351) will be possible in the future and states his premise that Olesha's stories "are constructed on a number of antitheses: idealism vs. materialism, vitalism vs. mechanism, romanticism vs. realism, traditionalism vs. futurism" (348).

34. Yuzovsky, "*Nepreodolennaia Evropa,*" *Literaturnaia gazeta*, 15 June 1931.

35. "*O Spiske blagodeianii Yu. Oleshi,*" *Na literaturnom postu* no. 28 (1931): 36.

36. Prozorov, "*O Spiske blagodeianii* Yu. Oleshi," 33–34. Prozorov is not completely unsympathetic to Olesha, and his article is accompanied on p. 35 by a humorous cartoon that depicts a rotund Olesha in Elizabethan garb holding a skull, presumably meant to suggest the skull of Yorick from Shakespeare's *Hamlet*.

37. Brown notes this ambivalence in *Meyerhold on Theater* (1969), 242.

38. See Rudnitsky, *Rezhisser Meierkhol'd*, 439.

39. Barratt, *Yurii Olesha's "Envy,"* 53.

40. Chudakova, *Masterstvo Yuria Oleshi*, 96.

41. Shklovsky, "*Struna zvenit v tumane,*" 201.

Chapter 4. Poetics as Counterpoetics

1. Quoted in Olesha's "*Avtobiografii 3,*" 524.

2. Clark's "Little Heroes and Big Deeds: Literature Responds to the First Five-Year Plan" (1978) is about official attempts to heroize Russian literature of the early 1930s.

3. See Olesha, "*O lise*" (1948), and the film scenario, *Devochka v tsirke* (1958). As Brumberg and Brumberg point out in *Vospominaniia o Yurii Oleshe*, 145, Olesha thought that everyone in a cartoon should speak in verse. In "A Little Girl at the Circus" the sparrows who visit the little girl use several rhymes of "*oi*" and "*ei.*" Olesha in his late reversion to "The Chisel" may have lacked the delicate touch needed for children's verse.

4. See *Ni dnia bez strochki, Izbrannoe* (1974), 494.

5. Mayakovsky is actually one of the best and most popular children's poets in the Soviet period. Elena Sokol analyzes and evaulates Mayakovsky's poetry for children in *Russian Poetry for Children*, esp. 152–66.

6. Shklovsky, "*Struna zvenit v tumane*," 203.

7. Robert Russell discusses the relationship between *No Day without a Line* and Kataev's *The Shattered Life* in *Valentin Kataev* (1981), 141–42. Kataev himself remarks in *Trava zabven'ia, Almaznyi venets* (1981), 440, that he has borrowed the phrase "the rose of a smile" (*roza ulybki*) from Olesha. See my introduction above for a discussion of Olesha's relationship to *My Diamond Wreath*.

8. Beaujour analyzes the relationship between Olesha's characters and Dostoevsky's underground men in "On Choosing One's Ancestors: Some Afterthoughts on *Envy*" (1979), 24–36. Tucker also notes this relationship in "Jurij Olesha's *Envy*: A Re-examination" (1982), 59.

Selected Bibliography

Works by Yury Karlovich Olesha

"*Angel.*" *Proletarii* 209, 210 (Kharkov). 14–15 September 1922. Rpt. in newspaper *RT*, 25 September 1966: 15.
"*Avtobiografiia.*" *Sovetskie pisateli* 3. Moscow: Khudozhestvennaia literatura, 1966: 517–26.
Autobiografiia. Tsentral'nyi Gosudarstvennyi Arkhiv Literatury i Iskusstva (Moscow). Fond 358, opis' 1, ed. khr. 21 June 1931.
"*Baski.*" *Vecherniaia Moskva.* 25 June 1937.
"*Bul'var.*" *Bomba* (Odessa) 11 (1917): 10.
"*Chernyi chelovek.*" *30 dnei* 6 (1932): 27–31.
Complete Short Stories and Three Fat Men. Transalted Aimée Anderson. Ann Arbor, MI: Ardis, 1979.
Devochka v tsirke. Fil'my-skazki. Stsenarii risovannykh fil'mov 5. Moscow: *Iskusstvo,* 1958. 49–77.
"*Diskobol.*" *Literaturnaia gazeta.* 28 June 1934. Excerpt from scenario that became *Strogii yunosha.*
"*Dvor korolia poetov.*" *Ogon'ki* (Odessa) 29 (November 1918): 1.
"*Gaskoniia.*" *Mysl'* (Odessa) 2 (1918): 1.
"*. . . I ty chast' istorii.*" Published O. Suok-Olesha. *Literaturnaia gazeta.* 4 August 1976.
Igra v plakhu. Trudiashchii mir (Kharkov) 1 (1922): 24–43. Rpt. in *30 dnei* 5 (1934): 35–48.
Izbrannoe. Introduction Viktor Shklovsky. Commentary V. Badikov. Moscow: Khudozhestvennaia literatura, 1974.
Izbrannoe. Zavist' i drugie. Russian Studies Series 72. Pullman, MI: Russian Language Specialties, 1973.
"*Kak eto proiskhodit.*" *Bomba* (Odessa) 14 (1917).
"*Kardinal'nye voprosy.*" *30 dnei* 12 (1935): 45–50.
"*Khrustal'nyi kubok.*" *Moskovskii bol'shevik.* 16 October 1945.
"*Koe-chto iz sekretnykh zapisei poputchika Zanda.*" *30 dnei* 1 (1932): 11–17.
"*Kogda vechernii chai s varen'em . . .*" *Ogon'ki* (Odessa) 7 (June 1918): 11.

"*Komsomol'ke* Chernovoi." *Molodaia gvardiia* 4 (1935): 159–60.
Malen'kii leitenant. With V. Riskind. *K pobede. Sbornik oboronnykh proizvedenii sovetskikh pisatelei Turkmenii.* Ashkhabad, 1942. 56–71.
"*Na matche.*" *Vecherniaia Moskva.* 19 September 1936.
"*Neizvestnye stranitsy izvestnoi knigi. Ni dnia bez strochki.*" Prefatory remark by O. Suok-Olesha. *Literaturnaia gazeta.* 19 September 1973.
"*Neobkhodimost' perestroiki mne yasna.*" *30 dnei* 5 (1932): 67–68.
Ni dnia bez strochki. Iz zapisnykh knizhek. Moscow: Sovetskaia Rossiia, 1965.
No Day Without a Line. Trans., ed., and intro. Judson Rosengrant. Ann Arbor, MI: Ardis, 1979.
"*Novyi chelovek—chelovek bor'by.*" From speech in *Chernomors'ka komuna,* 27 September 1934. *Voprosy literatury* 8 (1984): 180–84.
"*O lise.*" Illustrated A. Brei. Moscow: Krasnogvardeiskogo raipromtresta, 1948.
"*O malen'kikh p'esakh.*" *30 dnei* 8 (1933): 64–65.
Ogon'. Iz istorii kino 6: 65–87. Moscow, 1965.
P'esy. Stat'i o teatre i dramaturgii. Moscow: Iskusstvo, 1968.
"*Petr I.*" *Izvestiia.* 2 September 1937.
"*Piatyi god.*" *Bomba* (Odessa) 7 (1917): 7.
"*Pis'mo iz Odessy.*" *30 dnei* (1935): 71–73.
"*Pis'mo ot isterichnoi zhenshchiny.*" *Bomba* (Odessa) 10 (1917): 4.
Povesti i rasskazy. Moscow: Khudozhestvennaia literatura, 1965.
"*Pushkin.*" *Ogon'ki* (Odessa) 1 (May 1918): 5.
Saliut. Stikhi (1923–1926). Moscow: Gudok, 1927.
Stikhotvoreniia 1917–1921. Tsentral'nyi Gosudarstvennyi Arkhiv Literatury i Iskusstva, fond 358.
"*Udivitel'nyi perekrestok.*" *Ogonek* 44 (1947): 17.
"*V den' vyborov.*" *Literaturnaia gazeta.* 15 December 1937.
"*Val'ter.*" With A. Macheret. *Zvezda* 4 (1937): 14–45.
"*Velikoe narodnoe iskusstvo.*" *Literaturnaia gazeta.* 20 March 1936.
"*Videt' mir kak by vpervye.*" Published O. Suok-Olesha. *Literaturnaia gazeta.* 24 January 1973.
Yury Olesha. The Complete Plays. Ed. and trans. Michael Green and Jerome Katsell. Ann Arbor, MI: Ardis, 1983.
"*Zakaz na strashnoe.*" *30 dnei* 2 (1936): 33–36.
Zavist'. Illustrated Natan Al'tman. Moscow and Leningrad: Zemlia i fabrika, 1929.
Zubilo. Leningrad: Gudok, 1924.

Secondary Sources

Aborsky, Aleksandr. Untitled article. In Suok-Olesha and Pel'son, 186–202, q.v.

Anderson, Aimée, and Donald Anderson. Afterword to *Complete Stories and Three Fat Men*, by Yury Olesha. Ann Arbor, MI: Ardis, 1979.

Arutiunian, Yury. *Vsegda molodoi futbol.* Moscow: Moskovskii rabochii, 1984.

Avins, Carol. "Eliot and Olesha: Versions of Anti-Hero." *Canadian Review of Comparative Literature* 6 (1979): 64–74.

Babel, Isaac. *Konarmiia, Odesskie rasskazy, P'esy.* Moscow: Khudozhestvennaia literatura, 1957; rpt. Letchworth, Herts: Bradda Books, 1965.

Badikov, V. V. "O stile romana Yuriia Oleshi Zavist'." *Filologicheskii sbornik* no. 5 (Alma-Ata, 1966): 54–62.

———. "Primechaniia." *Izbrannoe*, by Yury Olesha, 559–75. Moscow: Khudozhestvennaia literatura, 1974.

Bagritsky, Eduard. "Posledniaia noch'." *Stikhotvoreniia i poemy*, 496–97. Moscow-Leningrad: Biblioteka poeta, 1964.

Bagritsky, Vsevolod. *Dnevniki, pis'ma, stikhi.* Compiled by L. G. Bagritsky and E. G. Bonner. Moscow: Sovetskii pisatel', 1964.

Bakhtin, Mikhail. *Problemy poetiki Dostoevskogo.* 4th ed. Moscow: Sovetskaia Rossiia, 1979.

———. *Rabelais and His World.* Translated by Helene Iswolsky. Cambridge: MIT Press, 1968.

———. *The Dialogic Imagination: Four Essays by M. M. Bakhtin.* Edited by Michael Holquist. Translated by Caryl Emerson and Michael Holquist. Austin: University of Texas Press, 1981.

Bakhtin, M. M., and P. N. Medvedeev. *The Formal Method in Literary Scholarship: A Critical Introduction to Sociological Poetics.* Translated by Albert J. Wehrle. Foreword by Wlad Godzich. Cambridge: Harvard University Press, 1985.

Barratt, Andrew. *Yurii Olesha's "Envy."* Birmingham Slavonic Monographs, no. 12. Birmingham, 1981.

———. "Yury Olesha's Three Ages of Man: A Close Reading of 'Liompa.'" *Modern Language Review*, 75, pt. 3 (July 1980): 598–614.

Beaujour, Elizabeth Klosty. "On Choosing One's Ancestors: Some Afterthoughts on *Envy*." *Ulbanelus Review* 2, no. 1 (Fall 1979): 24–36.

_____. "Proust-*Envy*: Fiction and Autobiography in the Works of Olesha." *Studies in Twentieth Century Literrture* no. 2 (Spring 1977): 123–34.

_____. *The Invisible Land: A Study of the Artistic Imagination of Iurii Olesha.* New York: Columbia University Press, 1970.

Belinkov, Arkadii. "*Poet i tolstiak.*" Part 1. *Baikal* no. 1 (1968): 103–10.

_____. "*Poet i tolstiak.*" Part 2. *Baikal* no. 2 (1968): 100–110.

_____. *Sdacha i gibel' sovetskogo intelligenta. Yurii Olesha.* Prepared for publication N. Belinkova. Madrid, 1976.

_____. "The Soviet Intelligentsia and the Socialist Revolution: On Yury Olesha's 'Envy.' " Part I. *The Russian Review* 30, no. 4 (October 1971): 356–68.

_____. "The Soviet Intelligentsia and the Socialist Revolution: On Yury Olesha's 'Envy'." Part 2. *The Russian Review* 31, no. 1 (January 1972): 25–37.

Berczynski, T. S. "Kavalerov's Monologue in *Envy*: A Baroque Soliloquy." *Russian Literature Triquarterly* no. 1 (Fall 1971): 375–85.

Berezak, I. "*Skazka o dvukh krysakh.*" Account of oral story by Olesha. *Neva* no. 3 (1977): 204–5.

Bialik, B. "*Iskusstvo ne byt' slishkom skuchnym.*" *Voprosy literatury* no. 7 (1981): 289–97.

Bjorling, Fiona. "Verbal Aspect and Narrative Perspective in Olesha's '*Liompa*'." *Russian Literature* 9, no. 2 (1981): 133–61.

Bobovich, Boris. Untitled article. In Suok-Olesha and Pel'son, 22–26, q.v.

Boichevsky, V. "*Kakoi ne dolzhna byt' kniga dlia detei.*" *Chitatel' i pisatel'*, 9 December 1928.

Bondarin, Sergei. *Gvozd' vinograda. Zapiski. Rasskazy. Povesti.* Moscow: Sovetskii pisatel', 1964.

Brown, Edward, ed. and trans. *Meyerhold on Theater.* New York: Hill and Wang, 1969.

Brown, Edward J. *Russian Literature Since the Revolution.* Rev. ed. New York: Collier Books, 1973.

Brumberg, V., and Z. Brumberg. Untitled article. In Suok-Olesha and Pel'son, 145–48, q.v.

Bulgakov, Mikhail. *Master i Margarita. Belaia gvardiia. Teatral'nyi roman.* Moscow: Khudozhestvennaia literatura, 1973, 423–812.

_____. *Sbornik rasskazov.* New York: Chekhov Publishing House, 1952.

Burke, Peter. *Popular Culture in Early Modern Europe.* New York: New York University Press, 1978.

Charnyi, M. *"Zagadka* Yuriia Oleshi. *Ushedshedie gody."* *Vospominaniia i ocherki.* Moscow: Sovetskii pisatel', 1967.

Chudakova, M. O. *Masterstvo Yuriia Oleshi.* Moscow: Nauka, 1972.

_____. *"Poetika* Yuriia Oleshi." *Voprosy literatury* no. 4 (1968): 120–35.

Chukovsky, Kornei. *Chukokala.* Moscow: Iskusstvo, 1979.

Clark, Katerina. "Little Heroes and Big Deeds: Literature Responds to the First Five-Year Plan." In *Cultural Revolution in Russia 1928–1931,* edited by Sheila Fitzpatrick, 189–206. Bloomington: Indiana University Press, 1978.

Clark, Katerina, and Michael Holquist. *Mikhail Bakhtin.* Cambridge: Harvard University Press, 1984.

Cornwell, Neil. "The Principle of Distortion in Olesha's *Envy." Essays in Poetics* 5, no. 1 (1980): 15–35.

_____. "Olesha's 'Envy'." *The Structural Analysis of Russian Narrative Fiction. Essays in Poetics* 1, edited by Joe Andrew and Christopher Pike, 115–36. Keele: Department of Russian Studies, Keele University (1976).

Croft, Lee B. "Charlie Chaplin and Olesha's *Envy." CLA Journal* 21, no. 4 (June 1978): 525–37.

Dolinov, G. I. *Vospominaniia ob odesskom literaturno-khudozhestvennom kruzhke "Zelenaia lampa."* Archive of the Saltykov-Shchedrin Public Library, Leningrad. *Fond 260, ed. khr. 1.*

Dzhandzhakova, E. V. *"O sochetaemosti slov v sovremennoi poeticheskoi rechi."* In *Voprosy yazyka sovremennoi russkoi literatury* edited by V. D. Levin, 401–15. Moscow: Nauka, 1971.

Ershov, L. F. *Sovetskaia satiricheskaia proza 20-kh godov.* Moscow and Leningrad: Akademiia nauk, 1960.

Esenin, K. *Moskovskii futbol.* Moscow: Moskovskii rabochii, 1974.

Flit, Boris. [Pseudonym *"Neznakomets."*] Editor. *Bomba* (Odessa) 30 (1917).

Freeborn, Richard. *The Russian Revolutionary Novel: Turgenev to Pasternak.* Cambridge: Cambridge University Press, 1982.

Galanov, Boris. *"Mir* Yuriia Oleshi." In *Povesti i rasskazy,* by Yury Olesha, 3–16. Moscow: Khudozhestvennaia literatura, 1965.

Gerasimov, Sergei. Untitled article. In Suok-Olesha and Pel'son, 98–104, q.v.

Gladkov, Fedor. Untitled article. In Suok-Olesha and Pel'son, 266–82, q.v.

Glan, I. Untitled article. In Suok-Olesha and Pel'son, 282–91, q.v.

Gorchakov, Nikolai A. *The Theater in Soviet Russia.* Translated by Edgar Lehrman. New York: Columbia University Press, 1957.

Harkins, William E. "The Philosophical Stories of Jurij Olesha." *Orbis Scriptus. Dmitrij Tschizhewskij zum 70 Geburtstag*, 349–54, edited by Dietrich Gerhardt et al. Munich: Wilhelm Fink Verlag, 1966.

_____ . "The Theme of Sterility in Olesha's *Envy*." *Slavic Review* 25, no. 3 (1966): 443–57.

_____ . "*No Day Without a Line*: The World of Iurii Olesha." *Russian Literature and American Critics. In Honor of Deming B. Brown. Papers in Slavic Philology* 4, 95–101. Edited by Kenneth N. Brostrom. Ann Arbor: University of Michigan, 1984.

Hoover, Marjorie L. *Meyerhold. The Art of Conscious Theater.* Amherst: University of Massachusetts Press, 1974.

Ingdahl, Kazimiera. *The Artist and the Creative Act. A Study of Jurij Olesha's Novel* Zavist'. Stockholm Studies in Russian Literature, no. 17. Stockholm: Almqvist & Wiksell International, 1984.

_____ . "The Life/Death Dichotomy in Jurij Olesha's Short Story 'Liompa.'" *Studies in Twentieth Century Prose*, 156–85. Stockholm Studies in Russian Literature, no. 14. Edited by Nils Åke Nilsson. Stockholm: Almqvist & Wiksell International, 1982.

Ivanova, E. M. "*Khudozhestvennoe edinstvo poslednei knigi* Yu. K. Oleshi '*Ni dnia bez strochki.*'" In *Nekotornye voprosy russkoi literatury XX veka*, 226–35. Moscow: Gosudarstvennyi pedagogicheskii institut im. Lenina, Kafedra sovetskoi literatury, 1973.

Ivask, Yu. P. Introduction. *Izbrannoe*. By V. V. Rozanov. New York: Chekhov Publishing House, 1956, 7–59.

Jones, Robert. "The Primacy of the Subjective in the Work of Jurij Olesha." *Melbourne Slavonic Studies* no. 3 (1969): 3–11.

Karelina, Tatiana. "*Seredina veshchei. Osobennosti poetiki skazki* Tri tolstiaka." *Detskaia literatura* no. 9 (1976): 18–20.

Kassil', Lev. *Sportivnye rasskazy.* Moscow: Fizkul'tura i sport, 1967.

Kataev, Valentin. *Almaznyi moi venets.* In *Almaznyi moi venets. Povesti*, 6–224. Moscow: Sovetskii pisatel', 1981,

_____ . "*Izgnanie metafory. Beseda s* V. Kataevym." *Literaturnaia gazeta*, 17 May 1933.

_____ . "*Proshchanie s mirom.*" *Sobranie sochinenii* 8: 436–38. Moscow: Khudozhestvennaia literatura, 1971,

_____ . *Razbitaia zhizn', ili Volshebnyi rog Oberona.* Moscow: Detskaia literatura, 1973.

_____ . *Sviatoi kolodets.* In *Almaznyi moi venets. Povesti*, 226–36. Moscow: Sovetskii pisatel', 1981.

_____ . *Trava zabveniia.* In *Almaznyi moi venets. Povesti*, 329–526. Moscow: Sovetskii pisatel', 1981.

Kazakevich, E. Untitled article. In Suok-Olesha and Pel'son, 292–94, q.v.

Kazansky, B. "*Priroda kino.*" In *Poetika kino,* edited by B. M. Eikhenbaum, 87–135. Moscow and Leningrad: Kinopechat', 1927; rpt. Berkeley Slavic Specialties, 1984.

Kharabuga, G. D. "*Fizicheskaia kul'tura v srednie veka.*" *Istoriia fizicheskoi kul'tury i sporta,* edited by V. V. Stolbov, 32–42. Moscow: Fizkul'tura i sport, 1983.

Kharms, Daniil [pseud. Daniil Ivanovich Yuvachev]. *Chto eto bylo.* Moscow: Malysh, 1967.

Komardenkov, Vasily. Untitled article. In Suok-Olesha and Pel'son, 39–42, q.v.

Kriger, Evgeny. "Yury Olesha." *Doroga k liudiam. Ocherki,* 161–169. Moscow: Sovetskii pisatel', 1978.

LeBlanc, Ronald D. "The Soccer Match in *Envy.*" *Slavic and East European Journal* 32, no. 1 (Spring 1988): 53–71.

Lepeshinskaia, O. Untitled article. In Suok-Olesha and Pel'son, 133–37, q.v.

Lidin, Vl. Untitled article. In Suok-Olesha and Pel'son, 169–73, q.v.

Livanov, B. Untitled article. In Suok-Olesha and Pel'son, 125–27, q.v.

Lunacharsky, A. V. "*Tolstiaki i 'chudaki'. Po povodu p'esy Oleshi v MKhat.*" *Sobranie sochinenii* 2, 426–68. Moscow: Khudozhestvennaia literatura, 1964.

———. "*Zagovor chuvstv.*" *Sobranie sochinenii* 3, 418–21. Moscow: Khudozhestvennaia literatura, 1964.

Luplow, Carol. *Isaac Babel's Red Cavalry.* Ann Arbor, MI: Ardis, 1982.

Maguire, Robert. *Red Virgin Soil: Soviet Literature in the 1920s.* Princeton: Princeton University Press, 1968.

Makhmudov, Kh. "*Zametki o tvorcheskom kontekste (k slovu . . .). Osobennosti yazyka i stilia* Yu. Oleshi *i* M. Zoshchenko." *Filologicheskii sbornik,* Vypusk 15–16, 3–17. Alma Ata: Izdanie KazGu, 1975,

Markov, P. Untitled article in Suok-Olesha and Pel'son, 105–19, q.v.

Matejka, Ladislav. Translator's Preface. *Marxism and the Philosophy of Language,* by V. N. Voloshinov. Trans. and intro. Ladislav Matejka and I. R. Titunik. Cambridge: Harvard University Press, 1986, vii–xii.

Mayakovsky, V. V. *Sobranie sochinenii.* 8 vols. Moscow: Pravda, 1968.

Meyerhold, V. E. *Stat'i, pis'ma, rechi, besedy.* 2 vols. 2: 1917–39. Moscow: Iskusstvo, 1969.

Morson, Gary Saul. *The Boundaries of Genre: Dostoevsky's* Diary of a Writer *and the Traditions of Literary Utopia.* University of Texas Press Slavic Series, no. 4. Austin: University of Texas Press, 1981.

Nikulin, Lev. Untitled article. In Suok-Olesha and Pel'son, 66–80, q.v.

Nilsson, Nils Åke. "A Hall of Mirrors: Nabokov and Olesha." *Scando-Slavica* no. 15 (1969): 5–12.

_____. "Through the Wrong End of Binoculars." *Major Soviet Writers: Essays in Critism,* edited by E. J. Brown, 254–79. New York: Oxford University Press, 1973.

Numano, Mitsuyosi. "Sud'ba iskusstva Yuriia Oleshi. *Ego zhizn' v metaforakh.*" *Novyi zhurnal* no. 145 (1981): 59–76.

Ovchinnikov, I. Untitled article. In Suok-Olesha and Pel'son, 43–54, q.v.

Ozerov, Lev. Untitled article. In Suok-Olesha and Pel'son, 231–41, q.v.

Panchenko, I. G. "*Problema garmonicheskoi lichnosti v romane* Yu. Oleshi Zavist' *i ego dramaticheskom variante* Zagovor chuvstv." *Voprosy russkoi literatury* 2, no. 24 (1974): 33–39.

Paustovsky, Konstantin. "*Chetvertaia polosa.*" *Sbornik vospominanii ob.* I. Il'fe i E. Petrove, compiled by G. Munblit and A. Raskin; edited by V. D. Ostrorogskaia, 80–92. Moscow: Sovetskii pisatel', 1963.

_____. Untitled article. In Suok-Olesha and Pel'son, 174–81, q.v.

Peppard, Murray B. *Paths Through the Forest: A Biography of the Brothers Grimm.* New York: Holt, Rinehart and Winston, 1971.

Peppard, Victor. "Olesha's *Envy* and the Carnival." *Russian Writers and American Critics. In Honor of Deming B. Brown. Papers in Slavic Philology* 4, 179–89. Edited by Kenneth N. Brostrom. Ann Arbor: University of Michigan, 1984.

_____. "Olesha's *No Day Without a Line:* A New Genre or an Old Trick?" *Proceedings of the Kentucky Foreign Language Conference 1985: Slavic Section* 3, 92–98. Edited by Boris A. Sorokin. Lexington: Department of Slavic and Oriental Languages, University of Kentucky, 1985.

_____. "Pil'njak's Use of Documents and Pseudo-documents in *Golyj god.*" *Russian Language Journal* 36, nos. 123–24 (Winter-Spring 1982): 143–50.

Perel', A. "*Pravoflangovye otechestvennogo futbola.*" *Stranitsy moskovskogo sporta,* edited by L. Budiak, 100–111. Moscow: Moskovskii rabochii, 1969.

Pertsov, V. *My zhivem vpervye: O tvorchestve Yuriia Oleshi.* Moscow: Sovetskii pisatel', 1976.

_____. "Yurii Olesha." *Poety i prozaiki velikikh let.* Moscow: Khudozhestvennaia literatura, 1969, 284–306.

_____. "Yurii Olesha." *Poety i prozaiki velikikh let.* Moscow: Sovetskii pisatel', 1976.

_____. Untitled article. In Suok-Olesha and Pel'son, 247–54, q.v.
Pil'niak, Boris. [Pseudonym Boris Vogau]. *Golyi god.* Letchworth, Herts: Bradda Books, 1966.
_____. *Mashiny i volki.* Munich: Wilhelm Fink Verlag, 1971.
_____. *Volga vpadaet v Kaspiiskoe more.* Moscow: Nedra, 1930.
Piper, D. G. B. "Iurii Olesha's *Zavist'*: An Interpretation." *Slavonic and East European Review* 47, no. 110 (1970): 27–43.
Polonsky, Viacheslav. "*Preodolenie zavisti.*" *Novyi mir* no. 5 (May 1929): 189–208.
Proffer, Ellendea. "On *The Master and Margarita.*" *Russian Literature Triquarterly* no. 6 (Spring 1973): 533–64.
_____. *Bulgakov. Life and Work.* Ann Arbor, MI: Ardis, 1984.
Prozorov, A. "*O Spiske blagodeianii* Yu. Oleshi." *Na literaturnom postu* no. 28 (1931): 33–41.
Rosengrant, Judson. Translator's Introduction to *No Day Without a Line*, by Yury Olesha, 11–26. Ann Arbor, MI: Ardis, 1979.
Rozanov, V. V. *Apokalipsis nashego vremeni. Izbrannoe.* Intro. and ed. Yu. P. Ivask, New York: Chekhov Publishing House, 1956, 379–406.
_____. *Opavishie list'ia. Izbrannoe.* New York: Chekhov Publishing House, 1956, 237–378.
_____. *Uedinennoe. Izbrannoe.* New York: Chekhov Publishing House, 1956, 193–236.
Rozanova, E. I. "*Proza Yuriia Oleshi.*" Dissertation, State University of Odessa, *Avtoreferat.* Kiev: Akademiia nauk Ukrainskoi SSR, 1968.
Rudnitsky, Konstantin. *Rezhisser Meierkhol'd.* Moscow: Nauka, 1969.
Russell, Robert. "Olesha's 'The Cherry Stone.' " In *Essays in Poetics, 1, The Structural Analysis of Russian Narrative Fiction*, edited by Joe Andrew and Christopher Pike, 82–114. Keele: Department of Russian Studies, Keele University, 1976.
_____. *Valentin Kataev.* Boston: Twayne Publishers, 1981.
Shishova, Zinaida. Untitled article. In Suok-Olesha and Pel'son, 27–38, q.v.
Shklovsky, Viktor. "*Glubokoe burenie.*" Introduction to *Izbrannoe, by* Yury Olesha, 3–10. Moscow: Khudozhestvennaia literatura, 1974.
_____. "*Iskusstvo kak priem.*" *O teorii prozy*, 7–23. Moscow: "Federatisiia," 1929; rpt. Ann Arbor, MI: Ardis, 1978.
_____. "*Mir bez glubiny.*" *Literaturnyi kritik* no. 5 (1933): 118–21.
_____. "*Poeziia i proza v kinematografii.*" In *Poetika kino.* Edited by B. M. Eikhenbaum. Moscow and Leningrad: Kinopechat', 1927; rpt. Berkley Slavic Specialities, 1984.

_____. "*Rabota* Yu. Oleshi *nad intsenirovkoi* Idiota." *Voprosy literatury* no. 5 (1973): 229–46.

_____. "*Struna zvenit v tumane. . . .* " *Znamia* no. 12 (1973): 194–204.

_____. Untitled article. In Suok-Olesha and Pel'son, 295–302, q.v.

_____. *Zoo or Letters Not about Love.* Translated by Richard Sheldon. Ithaca: Cornell University Press, 1971.

Shveitser, V. "Strogii yunosha." *Dialogy s proshlym,* 139–49. Moscow: Iskusstvo, 1976.

Sinyavsky, Andrei. [Pseudonym Abram Tertz.] *Mysli vrasplokh.* New York: Rauser Publishers, 1966.

Slavin, Lev. "*Na konchike lucha . . . K 80-letiiu so dnia rozhdeniia* Yu. Oleshi." *Literaturnaia gazeta,* 14 March 1979.

_____. *Portrety i Zapiski.* Moscow: Sovetskii pisatel', 1965.

_____. Untitled article. In Suok-Olesha and Pel'son, 3–21, q.v.

Smeliakov, Ya. Untitled article. In Suok-Olesha and Pel'son, 242–46, q.v.

Sokol, Elena. *Russian Poetry for Children.* Knoxville: University of Tennessee Press, 1984.

Solov'ev, Vladimir. "*Gulliver v strane velikanov.*" *Neva* no. 3 (1974): 163–66.

Sorokin, Boris. *Tolstoy in Prerevolutionary Russian Criticism.* Columbus: Ohio State University Press for Miami University, 1979.

Stacy, R. H. *Defamiliarization in Language and Literature.* Syracuse: Syracuse University Press, 1977.

Starostin, Andrei. *Vstrechi na futbol'noi orbite.* Moscow: Sovetskaia Rossiia, 1980.

_____. Untitled article. In Suok-Olesha and Pel'son, 55–65, q.v.

_____. "*Ya pomniu.*" *Yunost'* 5 (1983): 108–11.

Struve, Gleb. *Russian Literature under Lenin and Stalin, 1917–1953.* Norman: University of Oklahoma Press, 1971.

Suok-Olesha, O., and E. Pel'son, comps. *Vospominaniia o Yurii Oleshe.* Moscow: Sovetskii pisatel', 1975.

Szulkin, Robert. "Modes of Perception in Jurij Olesha's 'Liompa.' " *Studies Presented to Professor Roman Jakobson by His Students,* edited by Charles E. Gribble. Cambridge: Slavica Publishers, 1968.

_____. "The Artistic Prose of Jurij Karlovich Olesha." Dissertation, Harvard University, 1968.

Titunik, I. R. "Bakhtin &/or Voloshinov &/or Medvedev: Dialogue &/or Doubletalk?" *Language and Literary Theory,* edited by Benjamin A. Stolz, I. R. Titunik, and Lubomir Dolezel. 535–64. Ann Arbor: University of Michigan Press, 1984.

_____. Translator's Preface. *Marxism and the Philosophy of Language.*
By V. N. Voloshinov. Trans. and intro. Ladislav Matejka and I. R.
Titunik. Cambridge: Harvard University Press, 1986, vii–xii.

Todorov, Tzvetan. *Mikhail Bakhtin: The Dialogical Principle.* Min-
neapolis: University of Minnesota Press, 1984.

Tucker, Janet G. "Jurij Olesha's *Envy:* A Re-examination." *Slavic and
East European Journal* 26, no. 1 (Spring 1982): 56–62.

Tynianov, Yury N. *Arkhaisty i novatory.* Leningrad, 1929; rpt.
Foreword by Dmitrij Tschizhewskij. *Slavische Propaläen* 31.
Munich: Wilhelm Fink Verlag, 1967.

Uspensky, Boris. *A Poetics of Composition: The Structure of the Artis-
tic Text and Typology of a Compositional Form.* Translated by
Valentina Zavarin and Susan Wittig. Berkeley: University of
California Press, 1973.

Voloshinov, V. N. *Marxism and the Philosophy of Language.*
Translated with an introduction by Ladislav Matejka and I. R.
Titunik. Cambridge: Harvard University Press, 1986.

Wilson, Wayne. "The Objective of Jurij Olesha's *Envy.*" *Slavic and
East European Journal* 18, no. 1 (Spring 1974): 31–40.

Yuzovsky, Yu. I. "*Nepreodolennaia Evropa.*" *Literaturnaia gazeta.* 15
June 1931.

_____. "Evoliutsiia intelligentskoi temy: ot Oleshi do Finna." *O teatre
i drame. Stat'i. Ocherki. Fel'tony.* 2 vols., 1: 88–99. Moscow: Iskusstvo, 1982.

_____. *Vspominaia Oleshu. O teatre i drame. Stat'i. Ocherki.
Fel'etony.* 2 vols., 1, 338–45. Moscow: Iskusstvo, 1982.

Zamiatin, Evgeny. *Litsa.* New York: Chekhov Publishing House, 1955.

_____. *My.* New York: Inter-Language Literary Associates, 1973.

_____. *Povesti i rasskazy.* Letchworth, Herts: Bradda Books, 1969.

Zavalishin, Vyacheslav. *Early Soviet Writers.* New York: Praeger
Publishers, 1958.

Zoshchenko, Mikhail. "*O sebe, o kritikakh i o svoei rabote.*" *Mikhail
Zoshchenko. Stat'i i materialy,* edited B. V. Kazansky and Yu. N.
Tynianov, 8–11. Leningrad: Academia, 1928; rpt. Ann Arbor, MI:
Ardis, 1971.

Index

Starostin, Andrei, 3, 16, 48; on
  sport and soccer 4
Sterne, Laurence, 33
Struve, Gleb, 33–34, 47
Suok-Olesha, Olga, 9–10, 15, 25, 48
Swift, Jonathan: *Gulliver's Travels*,
  32
Symbolist drama, 47
Szulkin, Robert, 29

Technology, 15
Telegraph Building, 10
Thinking in images, 63–65
Tolstoy, L. N., 49, 69; *Anna
  Karenina*, 16, 139n.52;
  Childhood, 97; death of Ivan
  Ilich, 114; *War and Peace*, 21
TsDKA, 48
Turkistan, 14
Tverskoi Boulevard, 10
Twain, Mark: *The Prince and the
  Pauper* and *Tom Sawyer*, 127

Ugly duckling, 72
Ukraine, 4
Utochkin, Sergei, 3, 102–3

Visual perspective. *See* Optical
  perspective
Vitollo, Ernest, 49
Voloshinov, V. N., 18, 135n.62

Wells, H. G., 15, 129
The Whistle, 12. *See* Olesha: at
  The Whistle

Young Guard, 12
Yuzovsky, Yu., 120

Zamiatin, Evgenii, 21, 23, 35, 36;
  We, 23
Zhdanov, Andrei: and heroization
  of literature, 126
Zoshchenko, Mikhail, 50, 62, 127